Haydn Richards
Junior English 5
New Edition

Ginn is an imprint of Pearson Education Limited, a company incorporated in England and Wales, having its registered office at Edinburgh Gate, Harlow, Essex, CM20 2JE. Registered company number: 872828

www.ginn.co.uk

Text ©Haydn Richards, 1965

Revised edition 1997
This edition 2008

British Library Cataloguing in Publication Data is available from the British Library on request.

ISBN 978 0 435996 84 0

Copyright notice
All rights reserved. No part of this publication may be reproduced in any form or by any means (including photocopying or storing it in any medium by electronic means and whether or not transiently or incidentally to some other use of this publication) without the written permission of the copyright owner, except in accordance with the provisions of the Copyright, Designs and Patents Act 1988 or under the terms of a licence issued by the Copyright Licensing Agency, Saffron House, 6–10 Kirby Street, London EC1N 8TS (www.cla.co.uk). Applications for the copyright owner's written permission should be addressed to the publisher.

Typeset and illustrated by Planman Technologies India Pvt. Ltd.
Original illustrations ©Pearson Education Ltd, 2008
Cover design by Tony Richardson
Cover illustration ©Pearson Education Ltd, 2008

Acknowledgements
Every effort has been made to contact copyright holders of material reproduced in this book. Any omissions will be rectified in subsequent printings if notice is given to the publishers.

page 30 **A findforCarlos**
Just a Dog by Helen Griffiths.
By kind permission of Hutchinson Publishing Group Limited.

page 42 **Roger the dog**
What is the Truth? by Ted Hughes.
By kind permission of Faber and Faber Limited.

page 54 **Michael at the clinic**
Michael and the Music Makers by Harry Fleming.
By kind permission of the publishers, Brockhampton Press Limited.

page 60 **Sir Henry springs a visit**
Violet for Bonaparte by Geoffrey Trease.
By kind permission of Macmillan, London and Basingstoke.

page 66 **Lucy comes to Hagworthy**
The Wild Hunt of Hagworthy by Penelope Lively.
By kind permission of William Heinemann Ltd.

PREFACE

This new edition of Haydn Richards' popular series is for pupils studying in primary schools. Based on the revised 1997 edition, this new edition retains the excellent coverage of spelling, punctuation and grammar topics in each of the four books, as well as the wide range and varying complexity of the reading comprehension and vocabulary exercises.

In this new edition, key spelling, punctuation and grammar points and their examples are always highlighted in boxes on the page for quick and easy reference.

The Publisher

CONTENTS

Abbreviations	50, 83
Adjectives	
Comparison	8
Definition	3
Fitting into sentences	62
Formation	15, 20
Matching with nouns	3, 45, 62
Proper (countries)	27
Recognition	3
Adverbs	
Definition	43
Formation	43
Recognition	43
Agreement of subject and verb	69
Alphabetical order	11, 52
Analogies	80
Animal noises	77
Apostrophes	
Contractions	37
Possession	35
Capital letters	23
Collective nouns	19, 32
Comprehension	6, 12, 18, 24, 30, 36, 42, 48, 54, 60, 66, 72, 78, 84, 90
Contractions	37
Dictionary practice	13, 19, 31, 32, 50, 74
Diminutives	41
Direct speech	
Speech first	21, 25, 33
Speech last	21, 33
Several sentences	39
Interrupted	40
Direct to indirect	49

Several speakers	56
Doers of actions	81
Gender	13
Group names	29
Homonyms	64
Homophones:	
same sound, different meaning	16, 47, 71
Idioms	73
Indirect to direct speech	49
Letter writing	14
Noises of creatures	77
Nouns	
Abstract	32
Collective	19, 32
Common	32
Formation	4, 57
Gender	13
Kinds	32
Number	5
Possession	35
Proper	32
Recognition	1
vocabulary	1
Opposites	
Prefix dis	34
Change of word	38, 65
Paragraph topics	61
People	17
Prefixes anti, sub, tele	31
Proverbs	46, 87
Rhyming words	63, 76
Sentences	
Joining with who, which	44
Joining with conjunctions	55
The order of	82

    Subject and predicate   68
    Variety in writing   89

Silent letters   26

Similes   88

Sounds   79

Speech
    Direct   21, 25, 33, 39, 40, 49, 56
    Indirect   49

Synonyms   53, 74

Usage
    its, it's; passed, past;   10
    began, begun; broke, broken;
    came, come; whose, who's   51
    Revision   28

Verbal intelligence   9, 22, 59, 70, 86

Verbs
    Definition   2
    Fitting into sentences   2
    Participles   7, 58
    Past tense   7, 58
    Recognition   2

Words
    which save work   75

NOUNS

*The **detective** found a gold **watch**.*
Detective is the **name** of a **person**.
Watch is the **name** of a **thing**.
A **noun** is the name of a **person** or **thing**.

A Find the nouns in these sentences.

1. The box was made of wood.
2. The apples were put in a dish.
3. Milk turns sour in hot weather.
4. The lion slept in the shade under the tree.
5. Butter is made from milk.
6. It's dangerous to sharpen pencils with a knife.
7. These oranges are used to make marmalade.
8. Did you give the dog his food?
9. In winter the days are short and the nights are long.
10. The children enjoyed their visit to the zoo.

B These are the meanings of ten nouns, which are arranged in alphabetical order. Write these nouns.

1. a _ _ _ _
   the table in the most sacred part of a church
2. b _ _ _ _ _
   a hole in the ground made by a rabbit
3. c _ _ _ _ _ _
   a period of a hundred years
4. d _ _ _ _
   the name for a male duck
5. e _ _ _ _
   the overhanging edges of a roof
6. f _ _ _ _
   a short story with a moral
7. g _ _ _ _ _ _
   the tallest animal in the world
8. h _ _ _ _ _
   a tool for beating in nails
9. i _ _ _ _ _
   land entirely surrounded by water
10. j _ _ _ _ _ _ _
    the place where two or more railway lines meet

VERBS

*Wilson **trapped** the ball and **scored** a fine goal.*

The words **trapped** and **scored** tell us **what Wilson did**.

They are doing words, or action words, or verbs.

A **verb** is a word that shows **action**.

Examples

| trickled | shuffled | repaired | welcomed |
| sniffed | trampled | wriggled | galloped |

A Find the verbs in these sentences and write them in your exercise book.

Example 1 *washed   hung*

1 I washed the clothes and hung them on the line.
2 Although he tries hard he makes little progress.
3 Kai Man folded her sweater and placed it over the back of a chair.
4 When Penny had finished her breakfast she cleaned her teeth.
5 It takes Lee twenty minutes to walk to school.
6 Mina wrote the letter and James posted it.
7 I looked for my badge but it had disappeared.
8 The old man flopped down in the armchair and grunted.

B Fit the verbs in the list above into their proper places in the sentences below.

1 Miss Haines _____ the children to the party.
2 The dog _____ at the food before eating it.
3 Helen _____ across the field on her pony.
4 The worms _____ about in the rain.
5 William _____ the holes in the fence.
6 The rain _____ down the window panes.
7 Some of the audience _____ their feet.
8 The runaway horses had _____ on all the flowers in the park.

ADJECTIVES

> *Anne wore a **pretty silk** dress.*
>
> The words **pretty** and **silk** tell us something about Anne's dress.
>
> Because they describe the noun *dress*, they are called **adjectives**.
>
> *Sam ate **three** ice creams.*
>
> Numbers are **adjectives** too. **Three** tells us more about the noun *ice cream*.
>
> A word that **describes a noun** is called an **adjective**.
>
> *Examples*
>
> | | | | |
> |---|---|---|---|
> | valuable | loyal | nourishing | tedious |
> | thrilling | stormy | fatal | happy |
> | fashionable | savage | | |

A Make a list of the adjectives in these sentences.

Example **1** cold wet

1 It was a cold, wet night.
2 The two children played in the bright, warm sunshine.
3 The ancient castle was surrounded by a deep moat.
4 Hard work made him a successful man.
5 Justin wrote three long letters in one lonely hour.
6 Huge waves crashed on the stony beach.
7 Grandpa enjoys sitting by a warm fire in a comfortable armchair.
8 It was a delicious cake covered in thick chocolate icing.

B Use the ten adjectives in the list above to complete the phrases below.

1 a _____ meal
2 a _____ sea
3 a _____ child
4 a _____ ring
5 a _____ accident
6 a _____ skirt
7 a _____ lion
8 a _____ story
9 a _____ task
10 a _____ friend

C Write five sentences of your own using any of the completed phrases above. Phrases five and eight have been used in the examples below.

A fatal accident occurred at the corner of the High Street last night.

Roger read a thrilling story about pirates.

FORMATION OF NOUNS

Verb	Noun	Verb	Noun
admire	admiration	laugh	laughter
begin	beginning	lose	loss
compose	composition	move	movement
depart	departure	perform	performance
describe	description	permit	permission
divide	division	persuade	persuasion
exist	existence	please	pleasure
inform	information	rebel	rebellion
intend	intention	serve	service
invent	invention	suggest	suggestion
invite	invitation	treat	treatment

A Write the missing nouns that are formed from the verbs in bold type.

1 a clever ____ **invent** 6 faithful ____ **serve**
2 helpful ____ **inform** 7 simple ____ **divide**
3 hearty ____ **laugh** 8 a good ____ **begin**
4 a brilliant ____ **perform** 9 a life of ____ **please**
5 a serious ____ **lose** 10 an interesting ____ **suggest**

B Give the noun formed from the verb in bold type, which will complete each sentence.

1 The injured man found the least ____ very painful. **move**
2 It is our ____ to visit Greece next year. **intend**
3 Bad weather delayed the ____ of the plane. **depart**
4 Alan received ____ to leave school early. **permit**
5 The boy wrote an excellent ____ about dogs. **compose**
6 I have a deep ____ for the artist's work. **admire**
7 A hermit leads a very lonely ____. **exist**
8 Many were killed in the ____ against the government. **rebel**
9 *Treasure Island* contains a splendid ____ of Long John Silver. **describe**
10 After a little ____ Simon agreed to lend the boys his new football. **persuade**
11 The accident victim needed expert medical ____. **treat**
12 The ____ arrived in this morning's post. **invite**

NOUNS: NUMBER

Singular means **one**.
Plural means **more than one**.

Singular	Plural	Singular	Plural
girl	girls	leaf	leaves
book	books	lily	lilies
class	classes	hero	heroes

Some nouns have vowel changes in the plural:
Examples   man   men   tooth   teeth

Some nouns have such unusual plurals that you need to check them in your dictionary:
Examples   ox   oxen   child   children   louse   lice

Some nouns keep the same spelling for both singular and plural:
Examples   deer   swine   salmon   trout   sheep

These nouns have no **singular** form:
Examples   trousers   tongs   scissors   bellows   shears   tweezers

(A) Write the plural form for each of the singular nouns below. Follow the instructions on the left of each group.

	Singular	Plural		Singular	Plural
Add **-s**	chief	_____	Add **-es**	cargo	_____
	chimney	_____		echo	_____
	piano	_____		hero	_____
	roof	_____		potato	_____
				tomato	_____
Change **y** to **i**, add **-es**	battery	_____	Change **f** to **v**, add **-es**	half	_____
	hobby	_____		leaf	_____
	reply	_____		loaf	_____
	supply	_____		shelf	_____
				wolf	_____
Change the vowels	foot	_____	Use your dictionary	mouse	_____
	goose	_____		woman	_____

(B) Write the **plural** form of each noun.
1 half   4 sheep   7 leaf   10 wolf
2 hobby   5 bully   8 chimney   11 reply
3 potato   6 tomato   9 piano   12 goose

(C) Write the **singular** form of each noun.
1 feet   4 supplies   7 echoes   10 teeth
2 heroes   5 mice   8 women   11 batteries
3 loaves   6 shelves   9 toes   12 swine

SINBAD AND THE COCONUTS

One day a merchant gave me a large bag and advised me to go picking coconuts with some men whom we met in a place much visited by foreign traders. I kept close to the party until we reached the place where the coconuts grew.

The trees were so tall that I wondered how we should get the nuts, when the men, picking up some stones, threw them at the monkeys, of whom there were many on the branches. These creatures in return pelted us with coconuts, throwing them down so quickly that we soon filled our bags.

Day after day this was done until at length we had enough to fill the ship which waited for us in the harbour. Then, bidding the friendly merchant good-bye, I went aboard, and in due time arrived in Baghdad, none the worse for my adventures. I had done well, too, with my coconuts, having changed them for pearls and spices in the places at which we had called on the voyage.

The Arabian Nights

1 What did one of the merchants give Sinbad to carry the coconuts in?
2 Why did Sinbad wonder how they would get the coconuts off the trees?
3 Explain exactly how the men managed to get the coconuts.
4 When did the men stop collecting coconuts?
5 Where did Sinbad's voyage end?
6 In what way had Sinbad done well with his coconuts?

VERBS: PAST TENSE AND PAST PARTICIPLES

Learn the **past tense** and the **past participle** of the ten verbs in the first column, then do the exercises.

Present tense	**Past tense**	**Past participle**	**Present tense**	**Past tense**	**Past participle**
beat	beat	beaten	shake	shook	shaken
bleed	bled	bled	strike	struck	struck
catch	caught	caught	swim	swam	swum
forget	forgot	forgotten	throw	threw	thrown
hold	held	held	write	wrote	written

A participle always needs a helping word (an auxiliary verb).

The letter **was written** *neatly.*   The word **was** helps the participle **written**.

Learn the following auxiliary verbs:

was   have been   had   has been   were   had been

(A) Fill each space with the **past tense** of the verb in bold type.

 1 Philip _____ from the beach to the boat.   **swim**
 2 Arsenal _____ Chelsea by two goals to nil.   **beat**
 3 The Queen _____ hands with the General.   **shake**
 4 Adam _____ a letter to his uncle.   **write**
 5 His nose _____ badly when he fell.   **bleed**
 6 Stephen _____ the long pole with both hands.   **hold**

(B) Use the **past participle** of the verb in bold type to fill each space. The auxiliary verbs are underlined.

 1 The rider <u>was</u> _____ by his horse.   **throw**
 2 Donald <u>had</u> _____ to post the letters.   **forget**
 3 Chelsea <u>were</u> _____ by Arsenal.   **beat**
 4 Many books <u>have been</u> _____ about Napoleon.   **write**
 5 The English Channel <u>has been</u> _____ many times.   **swim**
 6 The old man <u>had been</u> _____ by his fall.   **shake**

(C) Write these sentences in past time by filling the spaces with either the past tense or the past participle of the verb in bold type.

 1 David _____ the ball.   **catch**
 2 The sheep were _____ firmly between the knees of the shearer.   **hold**
 3 Both boys were _____ by lightning as they sheltered under the tree.   **strike**
 4 I _____ my grandmother's birthday.   **forget**

COMPARING ADJECTIVES

Compare the heights of these three boys.

*John is **tall**.*

*Sam is **taller** than John.*

*Richard is the **tallest**.*

Taller is used when comparing **two**.

Tallest is used when comparing **more**.

In the examples above, **-er** and **-est** have been added to the word tall to show the comparative height of each boy.
There are many adjectives where **-er** and **-est** can be added without any change in spelling.
Examples   cold   col**der**   cold**est**
               clean   clean**er**   clean**est**

But look out for these spelling changes.
Drop **e** at the end
Examples   nice   nic**er**   nic**est**
               fine   fin**er**   fin**est**

Change the **y** to **i**
Examples   lazy   laz**ier**   laz**iest**
               shady   shad**ier**   shad**iest**

Double the last letter
Examples   thin   thin**ner**   thin**nest**
               slim   slim**mer**   slim**mest**

John   Sam   Richard

Ⓐ Use the correct form of the adjective in bold type to complete each sentence.

1. The monk's habit was made of the _____ material I have ever seen. **coarse**
2. This is the _____ classroom in the school. **cold**
3. Emily is the _____ of the two sisters. **old**
4. King Solomon was the _____ king who ever reigned. **wise**
5. Only the _____ ingredients are used in our cakes. **pure**
6. Jane chose the _____ slice of cake on the dish. **big**
7. High Street is a much _____ street than West Street. **wide**
8. Brighton is one of the _____ seaside resorts in Britain. **sunny**
9. Colin is the _____ of the twins. **naughty**
10. The oak is a _____ tree than the poplar. **shady**

WORDS TO COMPLETE WORDS

A Complete each unfinished word in these sentences by writing a word of **three letters** in place of the dashes at the beginning.

Example **1 bat bat**ch

1 The baker put another _ _ _ ch of bread in the oven.
2 Turn off the light. Do not _ _ _ te electricity.
3 A party of children sang Christmas _ _ _ ols to the old people.
4 It did not take the police long to _ _ _ ture the escaped convict.
5 The groceries are kept in a kitchen _ _ _ board.
6 Some _ _ _ tle were grazing in the field.
7 The footballer scored from a _ _ _ alty kick.
8 One stag had broken an _ _ _ ler in the fight.
9 The conjurer made the handkerchief _ _ _ ish.

B Complete each unfinished word below by writing a word of three letters in place of the dashes at the end.

Example **1 den bur**den

1 A big bur _ _ _ was placed on the camel's back.
2 Roy used a mag _ _ _ to pick up the nails he had dropped.
3 One of the knights was killed in the com _ _ _.
4 Mandy felt very tired after her swimming les _ _ _.
5 The frog gave a loud cr _ _ _ and hopped away.
6 King John was a tyr _ _ _.
7 The sudden light made him bl _ _ _ his eyes.
8 The gunners were right on the tar _ _ _.
9 Jill did not man _ _ _ to finish her homework.
10 The floor of the lounge was covered with thick car _ _ _.

USING WORDS CORRECTLY

Past often follows a verb, like ran **past**, flew **past**, went **past**, marched **past**, etc.

Examples
*I asked Ken to **pass** the jam.*
*Ken **passed** the jam.*

Examples
*It is **past** ten o'clock.*
*We walked **past** the new shop.*
*He had been ill for the **past** few days.*

It's means **It is**.
The ' shows that the **i** in **is** has been left out.

Example
***It's** not fair.*

Its means **'belonging to it'**.
Its shows **possession**.

Example
*The dog wagged **its** tail.*

(A) Copy these sentences, filling each blank with **past** or **passed**.

1. Helen ____ the cakes to Angela.
2. It was ten minutes ____ two when the train arrived.
3. Megan ____ her music examination with honours.
4. The colonel saluted as he ____ the Union Jack.
5. The colonel saluted as he marched ____ the Union Jack.
6. William hopes to do better in the future than he has done in the ____.
7. On the last lap Ahmed ____ all the other competitors and won easily.
8. On the last lap Ahmed sprinted ____ all the other competitors and won easily.

(B) Copy these sentences, inserting **it's** or **its** as required.

1. The rook flapped ____ wings and flew off.
2. I think ____ going to be a fine day.
3. Dad says ____ a long journey to London.
4. The little lamb frisked around ____ mother.
5. The kangaroo carries ____ young in a pouch.
6. Farmer Gray says ____ cold enough to snow.
7. The dog hurt ____ paw yesterday, but ____ all right now.
8. ____ time the puppy had ____ food.
9. ____ a pity that you missed my birthday party.
10. ____ not my fault that you got into trouble.
11. The parrot has lost ____ voice.
12. ____ too late now.

ALPHABETICAL ORDER

A Write the names of the eight objects in this picture in alphabetical order.

B Arrange the words in each group in alphabetical order. Look at the **first** letter of each word.

1 doubt	**2** justice	**3** month
youth	grab	unicorn
broad	kneel	skilful
active	chemist	nothing
lenient	eastern	haughty

C Look at the **second** letter of each word when arranging them alphabetically.

1 plank	**2** clever	**3** grape
press	crisp	geese
panic	centre	guilty
punch	canter	gander
perch	cheat	goose

D Look at the **third** letter of each word when arranging each group in alphabetical order.

1 decide	**2** harmful	**3** prune
demand	habit	prepare
deadly	haunt	produce
defeat	hatch	price
debtor	hamper	prank

THE CROWS AND THE SNAKE

Long ago, in India, a pair of crows nested in a hollow tree at the bottom of which lived a fierce snake which used to eat the young birds as soon as they were hatched.

"Oh dear, how can we stop this horrid snake eating our children?" said the mother crow one day.

"We must get rid of him, my dear," replied the father crow.

"But that is impossible," said Mrs Crow. "You know very well that he is much stronger than we are."

"Don't worry, my dear," answered her husband. "Just leave everything to me."

The following day the King's son came down to a nearby river to swim. No sooner had he entered the water than the father crow seized the lovely gold anklet which the prince had taken off and dropped it inside the hollow tree in which the crows had their nest.

When he was dressing, the prince noticed his precious anklet was missing and ordered his servants to search everywhere for it. After some time the missing anklet was found in the hollow tree. The servants also found the cruel snake and killed it, and so the crows were able to bring up their next family in peace.

This fable teaches us that skill will often make up for lack of strength.

1. Why were the crows unable to bring up a family?
2. Why did the mother crow think that they could not get rid of their enemy?
3. Who came down to the river the following day?
4. Why did he come?
5. What did the crow take when the prince was swimming?
6. Where did he hide it?
7. What did the servants find in addition to what they were looking for?
8. Why were the crows able to bring up their family in peace after this?

GENDER

A **boy** is a **male**.
A **girl** is a **female**.
The grouping of words according to sex is called **gender**.
Nouns that name **males** belong to the **masculine** gender.
Nouns that name **females** belong to the **feminine** gender.

Examples

Masculine	Feminine	Masculine	Feminine
bridegroom	bride	hero	heroine
cockerel	hen	host	hostess
dog	bitch	landlord	landlady
duke	duchess	monk	nun
earl	countess	prince	princess
emperor	empress	son	daughter
fox	vixen	stallion	mare
gander	goose	tiger	tigress
headmaster	headmistress	uncle	aunt

A Write the **feminine** gender of:

1 hero
2 dog
3 fox
4 monk
5 prince
6 earl
7 uncle
8 son
9 headmaster
10 host
11 stallion
12 emperor

B Write the **masculine** gender of:

1 aunt
2 bride
3 goose
4 hen
5 empress
6 landlady
7 mare
8 headmistress
9 tigress
10 duchess
11 vixen
12 nun

C Change each noun of the **masculine** gender to the **feminine** gender.

1 The duke is eighty years old.
2 As the children passed, the gander hissed at them.
3 The rider led the stallion to the stable.
4 We were welcomed by the landlord of The Swan Hotel.

D Write the word that is missing from each sentence.

1 The _____ and countess are abroad on holiday.
2 There were three hens and a _____ in the farmyard.
3 The _____ waited in vain for the bride to arrive at the church.
4 There were four puppies; one bitch and three _____.

E Masculine or feminine?
Use your dictionary to find out.

1 heifer   2 colt   3 widower

LETTER WRITING

Points to remember:

1 Write freely, as if you were actually **speaking** to the person to whom you are writing.

2 Write plainly and neatly.

3 See that your spelling is correct. If in doubt, use a dictionary.

4 Use a suitable ending:

| Parent | Love |
| Friend or relative | Best wishes
All the best
Love |

5 Address your envelope fully and plainly, so that the postman will have no difficulty in delivering it.

Here are some suggestions for letters, but you may choose something else if you wish. Write a letter to one of the following:

- A friend who has moved to another town and has just written to you.
- An uncle, thanking him for a birthday present he has sent you.
- A friend, describing a seaside holiday you are enjoying.
- A cousin, inviting him or her to spend a holiday at your home.
- A friend who is in hospital.
- Your mother, thanking her for a parcel she has sent you whilst you are away from home.
- A friend, congratulating him or her on passing an examination.
- A new penfriend, describing yourself, your family and your interests.

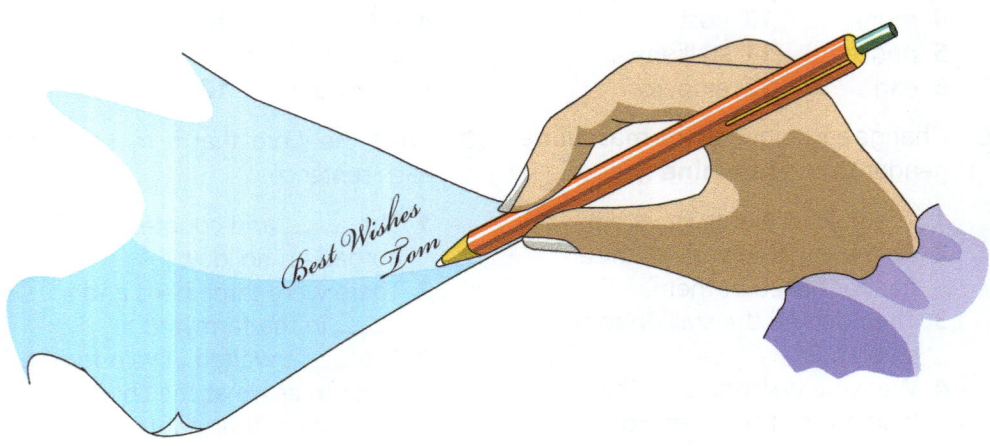

FORMATION OF ADJECTIVES

Many adjectives are formed by adding the letter **y** to a noun.

Examples   greed   greed**y**   rust   rust**y**   health   health**y**

In the examples above, **y** can be added to the noun without any change in spelling. But look out for the following changes.

If the noun ends with **e**, this letter is dropped before the **y** is added.

Examples   bone   bon**y**   noise   nois**y**   haste   hast**y**

When **y** is added to some nouns the last letter is doubled.

Examples   fur   furr**y**   mud   mudd**y**   skin   skinn**y**

A Form adjectives from the nouns in bold type. No change.

1. A person with a great **thirst** is _____.
2. A child who is longing to **sleep** is _____.
3. Fingers stained with **ink** are _____.
4. A sky with a lot of **cloud** is _____.
5. A loaf with a crisp **crust** is _____.
6. A sea with a **storm** raging is _____.

B Form adjectives from the nouns in bold type. Drop the **e**.

1. Water which is as cold as **ice** is _____.
2. Cheeks like a **rose** are _____.
3. An orange full of **juice** is _____.
4. A tree that provides **shade** is _____.
5. A chimney that pours out **smoke** is _____.
6. Hands covered with **grease** are _____.

C Form adjectives from the nouns in bold type. Double the last letter.

1. A road covered with **mud** is _____.
2. A garden that gets much **sun** is _____.
3. Foods that contain a lot of **fat** are _____.
4. A day when there is a lot of **fog** is _____.
5. Trousers which are as loose as a **bag** are _____.
6. A story that causes **fun** is _____.

HOMOPHONES: SAME SOUND, DIFFERENT MEANING

The words in each pair are pronounced alike but are different in spelling and meaning.		**him**	e.g. Let him come
		hymn	a song of praise
		hole	an open place
ball	anything round; a large party for dancing	**whole**	all of it; complete
		leak	escape of gas, water, etc.
bawl	to shout loudly	**leek**	a vegetable
bean	a vegetable; a plant	**mail**	posted letters; armour
been	e.g. has been; have been	**male**	e.g. Boys and men are males
flour	finely ground wheat	**peace**	quiet; stillness; freedom from war
flower	a blossom		
grate	a fireplace; to scrape	**piece**	a bit or part
great	large; important		

A Choose the correct word from the pair above to complete each sentence.

1 flower   flour
The cook used self-raising _____ for the cakes.

2 whole   hole
The greedy boy ate the _____ cake himself.

3 whole   hole
The _____ in the pipe was soon mended.

4 great   grate
The strong wind made the door _____ swing on its hinges.

5 peace   piece
The mouse nibbled the _____ of cheese.

B To complete each sentence below you need a pair of words from the list. Be sure to put each word in the right place.

1 The cook had _____ slicing runner _____ for two hours.
2 Nobody got any _____ until the baby was given a _____ of chocolate.
3 John was pleased when the music teacher asked _____ to play the organ for the morning _____.
4 The little boy started to _____ when the dog ran off with his rubber _____.

PEOPLE

ancestor	A person from whom one is descended.
bachelor	An unmarried man.
bully	Someone who teases and ill-treats those weaker than himself or herself.
coward	One who lacks courage or is afraid.
daredevil	One who is recklessly daring.
martyr	A person forced to suffer or die for a belief.
orphan	A child whose parents are dead.
truant	A pupil absent from school without permission.
volunteer	One who offers to serve of his or her own free will.
widow	A woman whose husband is dead.
widower	A man whose wife is dead.

Learn the words in the list above, together with their meanings, then answer the questions below.

A Give one word for each of the following:

1 A pupil who stays away from school without sufficient reason.
2 One who gives a service without being compelled to.
3 A child whose parents are dead.
4 A man whose wife has died and who has not remarried.
5 A person who takes unnecessary risks.

B Complete each sentence with a word from the list.

1 My aunt was a _____ for ten years before she married again.
2 Simon says he will never marry and will be a _____ all his life.
3 The Duke of Marlborough, who won the Battle of Blenheim, was an _____ of Sir Winston Churchill.
4 A _____ is someone who is afraid of almost everything.

THE PRINCESS AND THE PEA

There was once a Prince who wanted to marry a real Princess. He travelled all over the world looking for one, but failed to find one, so he returned home.

One night, during a terrible storm, there was a knocking at the gate of the town, and the old King went to open it. It was a Princess who stood outside. And, oh dear, what a state she was in! The water ran down from her hair and her clothes into her shoes, but she said she was a real Princess.

"Well, that we'll soon find out," thought the Queen, but she said nothing. Instead she went into the bedroom and laid a small pea on the slabs of the bed. Upon these she heaped twenty mattresses and twenty eiderdowns. The Princess was to sleep there that night.

In the morning she was asked how she had slept.

"Oh, very badly," she answered. "I have scarcely closed my eyes all night. I lay on something hard, so that my body is all black and blue."

Everybody knew then that she was a real Princess because no one else would have felt the pea through all those soft mattresses and eiderdowns, and so the Prince married her.

1 What did the Prince wish to do?
2 Who arrived at the gate during the storm?
3 What small thing did the Queen put on the slabs of the bed?
4 What did she put on top of this?
5 How did the Princess sleep that night?
6 *Extended writing* Imagine you are the Princess. Describe your night at the palace, and how you felt.

COLLECTIVE NOUNS

Some nouns name a **group** or **collection** of things.
These are called **collective** nouns.

Examples

Collection	Collective noun	Collection	Collective noun
bees	swarm	islands	group
books	library	kittens	litter
cows	herd	musicians	group
corn	sheaf	monkeys	troop
cutlery	canteen	soldiers	regiment
elephants	herd	oxen	team
fish	shoal	flowers	bunch
friends	party	thieves	gang
furniture	suite	whales	school

(A) Write the missing words.

1 a _____ of cutlery
2 a _____ of corn
3 a _____ of friends
4 a _____ of elephants
5 a _____ of flowers
6 a _____ of thieves
7 a _____ of books
8 a _____ of bees
9 a school of _____
10 a team of _____
11 a shoal of _____
12 a suite of _____
13 a group of _____
14 a troop of _____
15 a litter of _____
16 a group of _____

(B) Write the collective nouns that are missing from these sentences.

1 The look-out sighted a _____ of whales in the distance.
2 A _____ of thieves held up the mail van and robbed it.
3 The explorer took photographs of a _____ of elephants.
4 A _____ of fish was approaching the trawler.
5 Each room in the hotel had a new _____ of furniture.
6 The heavy wagon was drawn by a _____ of oxen.
7 The Orkneys are a _____ of islands off Northern Scotland.
8 A _____ of bees had settled on an apple tree in the orchard.
9 The tabby cat was very proud of her _____ of kittens.

(C) Use your dictionary to find which collections these collective nouns refer to.

1 galaxy
2 orchestra
3 fleet
4 troupe
5 bouquet

FORMING ADJECTIVES FROM NOUNS

Noun	Adjective	Noun	Adjective
affection	affectionate	fury	furious
anger	angry	haste	hasty
centre	central	hero	heroic
courage	courageous	marvel	marvellous
custom	customary	music	musical
danger	dangerous	nature	natural
expense	expensive	poison	poisonous
fame	famous	value	valuable
favour	favourite	victory	victorious
friend	friendly	wool	woollen

A What are the adjectives formed from these nouns?

1 wool
2 haste
3 favour
4 nature
5 poison
6 affection
7 fury
8 hero
9 victory
10 centre
11 anger
12 marvel
13 custom
14 music
15 danger
15 expense
16 courage
17 friend
18 fame
20 value

B Write the adjective, formed from the noun in bold type, that will complete each sentence.

1 The captain's ____ conduct saved the lives of his crew.   **hero**
2 My ____ book is *Watership Down*.   **favour**
3 The Niagara Falls are a ____ sight.   **marvel**
4 The thieves stole a ____ diamond necklace.   **value**
5 The lady bought a very ____ fur coat.   **expense**
6 Grandpa was seated in his ____ armchair.   **custom**
7 Some plants bear ____ berries.   **poison**
8 Marcia's hair has ____ waves.   **nature**
9 Judith is a very ____ child.   **affection**
10 The lost boy was helped by a ____ policeman.   **friend**

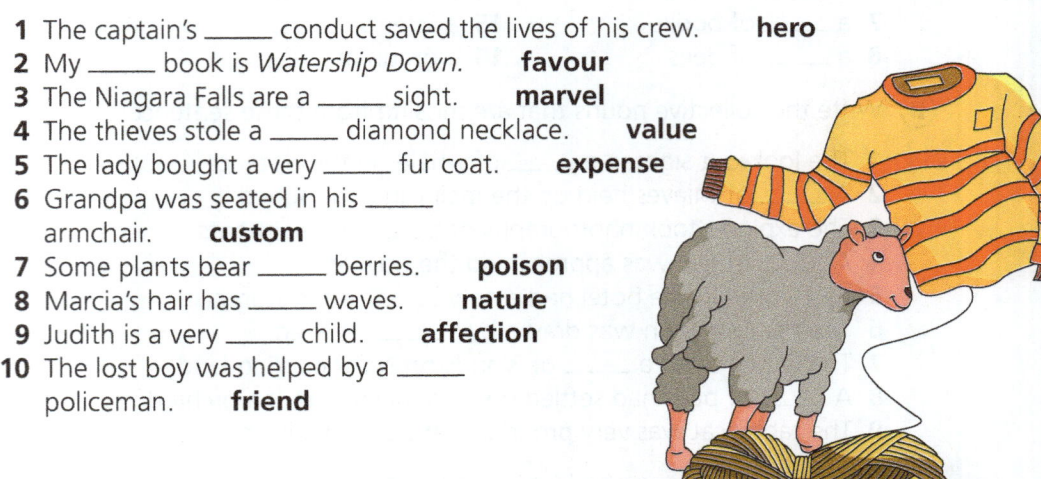

DIRECT SPEECH

> "**My bicycle has a puncture**," said Gary.
>
> In this sentence the **spoken words** come **first**.
>
> Gary said, "**My bicycle has a puncture**."
>
> In this sentence the **spoken words** come **last**.
>
> Notice the comma after **said** when the spoken words come last.
>
> Notice that the spoken words always begin with a capital letter, whether they come first in the sentence or last.

A Copy these sentences in your exercise book, putting in speech marks " " where required.

1. Nishani's mother warned her, Keep away from the fire!
2. The boatman shouted, Any more for the Skylark, please?
3. People in the audience were yelling, More! We want more!
4. Before leaving, Sally said, Thank you for a lovely holiday, Aunt Muriel.
5. Mr Paul asked, Will you play in goal, Tom?

B Rewrite these sentences so that the actual words spoken come last.

1. "I can't hear what you say," shouted Hari.
2. "Put your books away, everybody," said the teacher.
3. "My feet are icy cold," muttered the milkman.
4. "Would anyone like another cup of tea?" asked Mrs Gupta.
5. "Is this the way to the hospital?" enquired Richard.

C Rewrite these sentences so that the spoken words come first.

1. The showman shouted, "Three tries for 20p."
2. The old sailor remarked, "There's a big storm blowing up."
3. With a groan the full-back muttered, "I'm afraid my leg is broken."
4. Robin exclaimed, "Thank goodness there are no more exams!"
5. Janine's mother whispered, "Hush, David's sleeping."

FUN WITH WORDS

A In each group below, the second word of each pair is formed by writing a letter **before** the first word. A different letter is used for each group. Look at the letter that is added and write the missing words.

Example

ash	dash	ash	**d**ash
one	done	one	**d**one
rip	____	rip	**d**rip

In this group the letter **d** is added.

1 ale   tale   **4** hip   whip   **7** hop   chop
   ray   tray   arm   warm   lap   clap
   wine ____   edge ____   rash ____

2 end   send   **5** oil   boil   **8** air   fair
   ink   sink   lame blame   owl   fowl
   old   ____   rain ____   lock ____

3 ice   rice   **6** age   page   **9** elf   self
   oar   roar   our   pour   kid   skid
   each ____   lace ____   hark ____

B The first line of each pair below has a code word and its meaning. The same code is used in the second line of each example. You have to find out what this means.

Example   **1** *ijou* means **hint**
            uijo means **thin**

Using the code for the word **hint** we can find the meaning of the letters **uijo**.

1 ijou means **hint**   **6 ujef** means **tide**
  uijo means ____   **ejfu** means ____
2 dbsf means **care**   **7 bdut** means **acts**
  sbdf means ____   **dbtu** u means ____
3 ivct means **hubs**   **8 ebmf** means **dale**
  cvti means ____   **mfbe** means ____
4 nbsdi means **march**   **9 qfubm** means **petal**
  dibsn means ____   **mfbqu** means ____
5 tufbm means **steal**   **10 qjtupm** means **pistol**
  mfbtu means ____   **tqpjmu** means ____

USING CAPITAL LETTERS

Capital letters are used:	Examples
to begin every sentence	The pirate wore a big gold earring.
for the names of people and pets, and for initials	Mary, Ahmed, Spot, Fluffy, A. J. Compton
for the names of places, rivers, mountains, etc.	London, Snowdon, Thames, Niagara
in writing addresses	23 Second Avenue, Hopsham, Sussex
for the names of well-known buildings	The National Gallery, The British Museum, Windsor Castle
for the names of days, months and holidays	Thursday, January, Easter, Diwali
for the names of books, poems, songs, newspapers, etc.	Kidnapped, Watership Down, The Times
for the word I	When I bought it I thought I had a bargain.

A Rewrite these sentences using capital letters where required.

1 ian saw the houses of parliament and buckingham palace.
2 i shall be on holiday on saturday the 29th of july.
3 we are moving to 24 richmond road, swansea.
4 i saw anna and michael in the park, playing with their dogs digger and bonnie.
5 easter monday is the monday after good friday.
6 leah has read oliver twist and black beauty.

B Write the following:

1 three first names
2 three surnames
3 the names of three days
4 the title of any book

ALADDIN

In one of the large cities of China there once lived a tailor, whose name was Mustapha. Mustapha was very poor, and found it hard to provide food for himself, his wife, and his only child, Aladdin.

Aladdin was a very naughty and lazy boy. He would never do what his parents wanted him to do, but played in the streets from morning till night with boys who were as naughty as himself.

When Aladdin was old enough to learn a trade his father took him into his own shop and began to show him how to use a needle. It was no use. Aladdin had had his own way so long that he could not settle down to work. His father tried him over and over again, and was at last so angry and upset at his son's idle habits that he became ill and soon died.

The poor widow thought that her son would now earn a little money, but he would not. Aladdin was as idle as ever. In despair, she sold all the things that were in the shop, and with this money and the little she earned by spinning cotton she got on fairly well.

The Arabian Nights

1. In which country did Mustapha live?
2. How did he earn a living?
3. How many children did he have?
4. Name three of Aladdin's faults.
5. What did Aladdin do all day?
6. What did Mustapha do when Aladdin was old enough to learn a trade?
7. Why could Aladdin not settle down to work?
8. What effect did Aladdin's idle habits have on Mustapha?
9. What did Aladdin's mother do with the things in the tailor's shop?
10. How did Aladdin's mother earn money after her husband's death?

DIRECT SPEECH

"What is the matter?" asked Sam.

The words actually spoken by Sam were: **What is the matter?**

This is called **direct speech**.

These words are always written inside **speech marks**, or **inverted commas** " "

The first inverted commas " are placed **just before the first word spoken**.

The last inverted commas " are placed **just after the last word spoken**.

(A) Copy the following sentences, putting in the **speech marks**.
Remember that " comes after the comma or question mark, never before or above.

1 Pass me the butter, Carol, said her mother.
2 Would you like another cake? asked Mrs Brown.
3 These eggs are not fresh, complained the customer.
4 Is this the way to Norfolk, please? enquired the walker.
5 Look out below, shouted the steeplejack.
6 Please do all you can to help us, cried Old Tom.
7 The meeting is now closed, declared the chairman.
8 Pick your feet up, the sergeant-major shouted to the recruits.
9 I am the best bowler in the team, boasted Andrew.
10 Don't let me catch you throwing stones again, Peter warned his father.

(B) Copy these sentences, putting in all the punctuation and capital letters required.

1 you look tired said sarah
2 stop that thief shouted simon at the top of his voice
3 you can all have a rest now said mr palmer
4 has anybody seen my lunch-box asked matthew with tears in his eyes

SILENT LETTERS

Some words can be hard to spell because they contain silent letters.
Learn the words in these lists and then answer the questions in exercise A.

silent b	silent g	silent k	silent w
bom**b**	**g**nash	**k**nee	**w**rap
com**b**	**g**nat	**k**nife	**w**reck
crum**b**	**g**naw	**k**nit	**w**ren
lam**b**	**g**nome	**k**not	**w**riggle
thum**b**	si**g**n	**k**now	**w**rite

A Fill each space with the missing silent letter. Refer to the lists above.

1. A very small bird.   _ ren
2. A fairy who lives underground.   _nome
3. A tool with a sharp blade.   _nife
4. A small stinging insect.   _ nat
5. A tiny piece of bread or cake.   crum _
6. A baby sheep.   lam _

B Use your dictionary to find these words.

1. A bone in the finger.   knu _ _ _ _
2. A fold or line in the skin.   wri _ _ _ _
3. To use the hands to mix and squeeze ingredients.   kne _ _
4. Incorrect.   wro _ _
5. A person who repairs gas and water pipes.   plu _ _ _ _
6. Knotted and twisted.   gna _ _ _ _
7. A grave.   to _ _
8. A person from another country.   for _ _ _ _ _ _

PROPER ADJECTIVES

Learn these adjectives, which are formed from the names of countries. Notice that each begins with a capital letter.

Country	Adjective	Country	Adjective
Britain	British	Ireland	Irish
Canada	Canadian	Italy	Italian
England	English	Japan	Japanese
Egypt	Egyptian	Russia	Russian
France	French	Scotland	Scottish
Germany	German	Wales	Welsh

A What are the missing adjectives?

1 The Highlands of Scotland   the _____ Highlands
2 Goods made in Britain   _____ goods
3 Butter made in Ireland   _____ butter
4 A farmhouse in England   an _____ farmhouse
5 The language of France   the _____ language
6 Cotton grown in Egypt   _____ cotton
7 Ballet music of Russia   _____ ballet music

B In each line the missing word is the adjective formed from the name of the country in bold type.

1 Britain imports large quantities of _____ peaches. **Italy**
2 The travellers were stopped at the _____ frontier. **Germany**
3 Two girls were dressed in _____ costume. **Japan**
4 A great welcome awaited Solzhenitsyn, the _____ writer. **Russia**
5 _____ apples have a fine flavour. **Canada**
6 In the museum there is an _____ mummy. **Egypt**
7 The tourists spent a week in Paris, the _____ capital. **France**

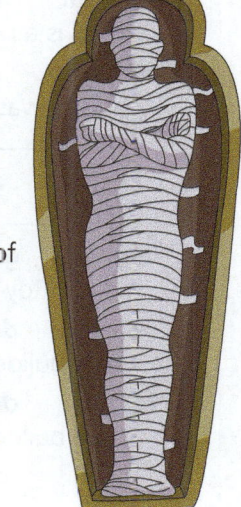

C Write six sentences of your own, each containing one of the adjectives formed from the names of these countries.

1 Wales   4 England
2 France   5 Ireland
3 Scotland   6 Britain

USING WORDS CORRECTLY: REVISION

A Select the word from those in bold type above each sentence that will complete each sentence correctly.

1 saw   seen
Several people _____ the accident.

2 saw   seen
Several people had _____ the accident.

3 is   are
There _____ a big crowd of people outside the shop.

4 is   are
There _____ crowds of people outside the shop.

5 to   too   two
I think _____ bags of potatoes are _____ heavy for you _____ carry.

B Select the word from those in bold type that will complete each sentence correctly.

1 eat   ate   eaten
The dog _____ all his food.

2 eat   ate   eaten
After he had _____ his food the dog slept.

3 taken   took
Several photographs of the wedding were _____.

4 taken   took
The photographer _____ photographs of the wedding.

5 hear   here
This is a radio programme everybody should _____.

6 there   their
_____ was great excitement when the team won _____ promotion.

7 give   gave   given
Roy _____ the books out and sat down.

8 give   gave   given
After Roy had _____ the books out he sat down.

9 did   done
The builders _____ their work well.

10 did   done
The builders have _____ their work well.

GROUP NAMES

buildings	months	games	rivers
counties	numbers	headgear	seasons
entertainments	occupations	letters	weapons

A Write the **group name** for the three things in each of the columns below. Look at the words in the list above.

1 summer	4 Kent	7 carpenter	10 April
winter	Surrey	miner	August
spring	Yorkshire	farmer	March
2 sword	5 circus	8 Thames	11 draughts
rifle	cinema	Severn	chess
bomb	theatre	Humber	dominoes
3 m t h	6 4 9 1	9 cap	12 hospital
l z e	12 35 67	hat	school
r q k		beret	museum

B In each column below choose the word that is the **group name** for all the other words.

1 fly	2 skylark	3 giraffe
wasp	swallow	animal
insect	robin	tiger
bee	bird	wolf
spider	nightingale	deer
gnat	sparrow	leopard

C Draw four columns and write the headings:

| **Fish** | **Flowers** | **Groceries** | **Trees** |

Then place the words below in their correct columns. There will be six words in each group.

beech	lard	herring	pansy
tea	elm	daisy	plaice
daffodil	hake	ash	sugar
salmon	bluebell	cheese	sycamore
butter	oak	tulip	cod
snowdrop	mackerel	birch	margarine

A FIND FOR CARLOS

The brindle puppy wandered on a little further, coming to a crack in the ground which was lined with a few blades of grass and wildflowers. A trickle of water drew her attention and at this she lapped, after half choking herself before realising how to use her tongue, and then she curled up on a patch of grass which had died in the sun and fell asleep.

It was there that Carlos found her later that afternoon. He lived in a block of flats beyond the cottages and had wandered that way out of sheer curiosity and boredom. Too new to the district to have made any friends, time lay heavily on his hands that Sunday afternoon. He was thirteen, too young according to his sixteen-year-old brother to share his pursuits; lonely.

He found the crack in the ground along which the narrow, dirty stream trickled and because there was a little bit of grass and a few flowers, he thought there might be frogs or lizards or something. When he first saw the brindle puppy he thought she was dead, but then he saw the tiny flanks heave and picked her up, his heart jumping with excitement at his find.

The deserted place, her bedraggled condition, made him sure that she belonged to no one. He pushed her inside his anorak and turned for home, his instinct being to get away from the place as soon as possible, just in case someone came for her.

Just a Dog Helen Griffiths

1. How can you tell that the puppy was very young?
2. What buildings did Carlos pass on his way to the puppy?
3. Why had Carlos wandered out that afternoon?
4. Why had he not made any friends?
5. Why did Carlos' brother not want his company?
6. What did Carlos expect to find in the crack?
7. How did he know the puppy was alive?
8. Why did he feel sure that the puppy had no owner?
9. Why did he want to go as soon as possible?
10. *Extended writing*
    Imagine you are Carlos. Where do you take the puppy? Describe what happens.

PREFIXES: *anti-, sub-, tele-*

You learned in Books 1 and 2 that a prefix is a syllable or syllables joined to the **beginning** of a word.

Learn these three prefixes. They will help you understand the meaning of quite long words. They will also help you to spell them correctly.

anti- means AGAINST

An **anti**septic prevents the spread of germs by acting **against** them.

sub- means UNDER

A **sub**marine is specially designed to be able to travel **under** the surface of the water.

tele- means FAR OFF

A **tele**vision set receives sounds and pictures from **far away**.

Use your dictionary to find out the meaning of these words.

A

1. antidote
2. antifreeze
3. anticlockwise
4. antibiotic

B

1. subway
2. submerge
3. subterranean
4. subside

C

1. telephoto lens
2. telescope
3. telephone
4. telepathic

D Choose one word from each of the three exercises above, **A**, **B** and **C**. Use each of the words you have chosen in a sentence.

NOUNS

You have learned that **nouns name** things.

There are four kinds of nouns, depending on the kind of things they name.

1 **Common** nouns name all the things you can see, hear, touch, taste or smell.
   Examples   book   music   apple
2 **Proper** nouns name all the things that have to begin with a capital letter.
   Examples   Monday   Anna   London
3 **Collective** nouns name collections.
   Examples   herd   swarm   galaxy
4 **Abstract** nouns name feelings and ideas.
   Examples   happiness   pride   intention

A Look around the room and write down five common nouns that name things that you can see.

B Do you know these proper nouns? Remember to begin each answer with a capital letter.

   1 Shakespeare's first name.
   2 The capital of France.
   3 The last month of the year.
   4 The highest mountain in the world.

C Use your dictionary to find out the difference in meaning between these groups of people.

   1 mob
   2 audience
   3 crowd
   4 congregation

D In the spaces write the abstract noun that can replace the words in bold type.

   1 Tell me **what you have decided**.
      Tell me your _____.
   2 **The way she behaved** was dreadful.
      Her _____ was dreadful.
   3 Everybody knows **what she plans to do**.
      Everybody knows her _____.
   4 Shushana was given an award for **being so brave**.
      Shushana was given an award for _____.

DIRECT SPEECH

> When we write the words spoken by someone we put **speech marks** round them. These are also called **inverted commas**.
>
> *Examples*
>
> "**P**lease shut the door after you," said Rodney irritably.
>
> The farmer shouted angrily, "**G**et out of the hayfield."
>
> Notice the capital letter at the beginning of a sentence of direct speech.
>
> Notice how " is used at the beginning of the words spoken and " at the end.
>
> Notice where commas are used in both examples.

(A) Copy these sentences and put speech marks round the words actually spoken.

1. Your shoelace is undone, Barbara, said Wendy.
2. Did you remember to bring a loaf, Sonia? asked her mother.
3. These cauliflowers were cut this morning, madam, said the greengrocer.
4. Keep him in bed for a few days, advised the doctor.

(B) Copy these sentences, putting speech marks and capital letters where required.

1. The dentist said, you should have that tooth filled.
2. Linda remarked, this is the tastiest meal I have had for a long time.
3. Handing him fifty pence, the old lady said, thank you for your help, my boy.
4. The auctioneer asked, is there any advance on fifty pounds?

(C) Copy these sentences, putting in all the punctuation that is needed. Use the two examples in the box at the top of the page as your guide.

1. i feel very thirsty said nasser
2. mr green replied you are always thirsty when it is time to do some work
3. that is very true agreed sarah
4. it is nothing to do with you retorted harry angrily

OPPOSITES: USING dis-

The opposites of some words are formed by writing **dis-** before them.

Examples

appear	**dis**appear
like	**dis**like
honest	**dis**honest
comfort	**dis**comfort

Remember that in writing **dis-** before **satisfied** the two letters **s** come together – **dissatisfied**.

A Write the opposites of these words by placing **dis-** before them.

1 agree
2 allow
3 believe
4 advantage
5 comfort
6 contented
7 favour
8 honest
9 like
10 loyal
11 order
12 pleased
13 respect
14 satisfied
15 infect
16 trust

B Rewrite these sentences, changing the words in bold type so that they will have an opposite meaning.

1 The baby proved to be a very **contented** child.
2 Many people **like** walking.
3 I **believed** everything he said.
4 The manager was **satisfied** with the week's takings.
5 The interviewer treated the old man with **respect**.

C Use one of the words beginning with **dis-** to complete each sentence.

1 A cashier who steals money from his employer is _____.
2 When something is to your _____ it is against your interests.
3 You _____ a person when you think he is telling lies.
4 Things are in _____ when they are not in proper order.
5 People _____ when they hold opposite views on any matter.

disappear

NOUNS: POSSESSION

The sailor used the foot of a rabbit as a charm.

*The sailor used a **rabbit's** foot as a charm.*

The 's in **rabbit's** shows that the foot belonged to a rabbit.

When a plural noun ends with **s** possession is shown by writing the ' after the **s**.

Examples

ladies' hats   the girls' bicycles

But note: *children's books*

Here the noun is plural but it does not end in **s**.

A Write the missing words.

1 the tail of a kangaroo
   a _____ tail
2 the wool of the sheep
   the _____ wool
3 the ears of a donkey
   a _____ ears
4 the beak of an eagle
   an _____ beak
5 the car of the woman
   the _____ car
6 the tail of a lion
   a _____ tail

B Give the missing words.

1 a school for boys   a _____ school
2 a nest belonging to robins   a _____ nest
3 a playground for girls   a _____ playground
4 a home for dogs   a _____ home
5 a camp for soldiers   a _____ camp
6 the trunks belonging to the elephants
   the _____ trunks
7 the tails of the cows   the _____ tails
8 a meeting for teachers   a _____ meeting
9 the treasure belonging to the pirates
   the _____ treasure
10 the burrows of the rabbits the _____ burrows

C Use each of these words in a sentence of your own.

cat's   girl's   horses'   boys'
cats'   girls'   nurse's   nurses'
horse's   boy's

PINOCCHIO AND THE POLICEMAN

Geppetto took the marionette in his hands and placed him on the floor to see if he could walk; but Pinocchio's legs were stiff. So Geppetto took him by the hand and showed him how to put one foot before the other. When the stiffness was out of his legs Pinocchio began to walk alone, and run round the room; and finally he slipped out of the door into the street and ran away. Poor old Geppetto ran after him as fast as he could, but he could not catch him, for the little scamp jumped like a rabbit.

"Catch him! Catch him!" cried Geppetto; but when the people saw that wooden marionette running as fast as a racehorse they stared at him in amazement, and then laughed and laughed until their sides were sore.

At last a policeman appeared. When he heard such a clatter he thought that somebody's horse had got away from its master; so he courageously planted himself in the middle of the street with his legs wide apart, determined to stop it.

While Pinocchio was still a long way off he saw the policeman barricading the street and he decided to run between his legs before he realized what he meant to do; but he failed dismally. The policeman, without moving from his position, picked him up neatly by the nose and returned him to Geppetto, who meant to pull his ears well to punish him for his naughtiness. Imagine, therefore, how he felt when he couldn't find any ears: and do you know why? Because he had made him in such a hurry that he had forgotten his ears.

The Adventures of Pinocchio   Carlo Collodi

1. Why did Geppetto place the marionette on the floor?
2. Why was Pinocchio unable to walk?
3. How did Geppetto help him to walk?
4. Where did Pinocchio go after learning to walk and run?
5. Why was Geppetto unable to catch him?
6. What did the people do when they saw Pinocchio running?
7. What did the policeman think when he heard such a clatter?
8. What happened to Pinocchio when he tried to run between the policeman's legs?
9. How did Geppetto intend to punish Pinocchio for running away?
10. Why was he unable to carry out this punishment?

CONTRACTIONS

The short way of writing **has not** is **hasn't**.

The short way of writing **you will** is **you'll**.

Remember that the apostrophe ' shows that some letters have been left out when the two words are joined together.

Now look at these words.

I am	I'm	I have	I've
you are	you're	you have	you've
we are	we're	we have	we've
they are	they're	they have	they've

These shortened words are called **contractions**. This is because they are **contracted** or **made shorter**.

(A) Write a contraction in place of the words in bold type in these sentences.

1 Thank you, **we have** had a lovely time.
2 I think **I am** getting slimmer.
3 The Joneses say that **they are** going to fly to Italy.
4 Please let me know when **you have** finished your work.
5 **I have** lost my stamp album.
6 Please tell Susan that **we are** ready to start.
7 We all miss you when **you are** absent from school.
8 **They have** been saving up to go to America for ages.

(B) Write the contractions for the following. Some are contained in Books 1 and 2.

1 they are   6 we will   11 we have   16 is not
2 it is   7 you have   12 they will   17 she is
3 I have   8 he is   13 you are   18 cannot
4 you will   9 we are   14 she will   19 he will
5 I am   10 I will   15 they have   20 have not

(C) Change these contractions back into two words.

1 isn't   2 he'll   3 it's

OPPOSITES

	opposite			opposite
above	below		deep	shallow
bright	dull		drunk	sober
busy	idle		foolish	wise
cheap	dear		rough	smooth
dead	alive		tender	tough

A Write the opposites of these words. You learned some of them in Book 2.

1 more
2 tender
3 quiet
4 sharp
5 busy
6 better
7 wise
8 heavy
9 wide
10 below
11 deep
12 evil
13 dull
14 kind
15 alive
16 awake
17 drunk
18 glad
19 cheap
20 rough

B Rewrite these sentences, changing the words in bold type so as to give them the **opposite** meaning.

Example   1   *Food is very **dear** in some parts of Europe.*
                  *Food is very **cheap** in some parts of Europe.*

1 Food is very **dear** in some parts of Europe.
2 The cotton mills have been **idle** for many months.
3 The lake was quite **shallow** in places.
4 In only one classroom was the temperature **above** freezing point.
5 The new pupil proved to be a **bright** boy.
6 Our Christmas turkey was very **tough**.
7 The shopkeeper was a very **foolish** man.
8 All the occupants of the boat were **dead**.
9 The police found that the motorist was **sober**.
10 The wood had a **smooth** surface.

DIRECT SPEECH

Practise all that you have learned about punctuating direct speech by punctuating these longer examples.

Remember that speech marks (inverted commas) show where each speech **begins** and **ends**.

Don't put speech marks around each sentence in a long speech.

Examples

"Please shut the door after you," said Rodney irritably. "I have a dreadful cold and you are making it much worse. You never shut the door when you go out."

"I do apologise. I didn't know that you had a cold," said Amelia. "I thought it was rather hot in here and that you would like some fresh air."

A Copy these speeches and put in the inverted commas where they are needed.

1 Today we have a visitor coming to speak to you, said Mrs Wallace. I hope you will listen carefully to what she has to say. You will have a chance to ask questions at the end of her talk.
2 I'm off to the beach for the day. Does anybody want to come with me? asked Uncle John. I'm leaving in half an hour and I can take two more people in the back of the car. Anyone interested?
3 Sooty is nearly 20 years old, said Anna. That's a good age for a cat. She's very healthy but she's not as energetic as she used to be.

B Copy out this speech. Put in all the punctuation that is needed.

my father takes us walking every sunday moaned kayleigh we have to walk for miles and miles across dartmoor i hate it but he still makes us do it walking makes me tired and bored id rather stay at home but he takes no notice

DIRECT SPEECH

You will notice in the stories you read that long sentences of direct speech are sometimes interrupted.

Example
"I am beginning to think," said Darren, "that you are a genius."

The sentence spoken by Darren is:

I am beginning to think that you are a genius.

The two parts of the sentence have speech marks around them when they are interrupted by **said Darren**.

Notice that no capital letter is needed when the spoken sentence is continued.

Notice how the commas are positioned.

A Copy the sentences, putting in the speech marks.

1 I will help you if I can, said my father, but I'm not very good at maths.
2 When we opened the door, whispered Amy, we saw the ghost!
3 Christmas won't be Christmas, grumbled Jo, without any presents.
4 Before you go out, said Sarah's mother firmly, you are going to tidy your room.

B Copy these sentences, putting in all the punctuation that is needed.

1 does anybody here shouted donna have a spare calculator
2 well grumbled jack you seem to have sorted everything out without me
3 i am not sure said miss macmillan that i want to hear any more of this story
4 in five seconds declared declan you will hear the clock strike
5 how many times do I have to tell you said mum crossly not to slam the door
6 watch out yelled the man on the ladder or youll tip me off
7 now my dear said the snow queen come inside my lovely palace
8 oh martin said sarah youve spoiled my painting now

YOUNG ONES

Learn the name of the young of each of these creatures, then answer the questions that follow.

Adult	Young	Adult	Young
bear	cub	goat	kid
cat	kitten	goose	gosling
cow	calf	hen	chick
deer	fawn	lion	cub
dog	puppy	sheep	lamb
duck	duckling	swan	cygnet
eagle	eaglet		

(A) What words are used for:

1. a young dog?
2. a young sheep?
3. a young lion?
4. a young cat?
5. a young goat?
6. a young duck?
7. a young cow?
8. a young hen?
9. a young eagle?
10. a young deer?
11. a young bear?
12. a young swan?
13. a young goose?

(B) Write the word that is required to complete each of these sentences.

1. The lioness at the zoo gave birth to two _____.
2. Our spaniel is kept busy looking after her mischievous _____.
3. Betty, the Persian cat, carried one of her _____ in her mouth.
4. The little _____ were sheltering beneath the mother hen's wings.
5. The little _____ followed the mother sheep wherever she went.
6. The nanny-goat and her two _____ were lying down in the field.
7. Followed by her five fluffy yellow _____, the mother duck waddled happily about the farmyard.
8. The eagle dropped the food she had brought right into the open mouths of her _____.
9. The cow mooed loudly for her _____, which had gone astray.
10. In the park we saw a graceful deer and her lovely little _____.

ROGER THE DOG

Asleep he wheezes at his ease.
He only wakes to scratch his fleas.

He hogs the fire, he bakes his head
As if it were a loaf of bread.

He's just a sack of snoring dog.
You can lug him like a log.

You can roll him with your foot,
He'll stay snoring where he's put.

I take him out for exercise,
He rolls in cowclap up to his eyes.

He will not race, he will not romp,
He saves his strength for gobble andchomp.

He'll work as hardas you couldwish
Emptying his dinner dish,

Then flops flat, and digs down deep,
Like a miner, into sleep.

Ted Hughes

1. What does Roger save his strength for?
2. What evidence is there in the poem that Roger sleeps very deeply?
3. How many words can you find in verse one with a long **ee** sound?
4. What makes you feel that Roger is not the kind of dog that would enjoy chasing rabbits?
5. What does the expression "hogs the fire" (in verse two) mean?
6. Alliteration is when two or more words begin with the same letter, like **d**igs and **d**eep in the last verse. Find three other examples of alliteration that you like in this poem.
7. There are lots of good comparisons in this poem. Make a list of all that you can find. Which one do you like best and why?
8. Would you like to have Roger as your pet? Give your reasons for saying "yes" or "no".

ADVERBS

Bill walked **slowly** down the lane.

The word **slowly** tells us **how** Bill walked.

He could have walked in several different ways, each of which could be described by one word:

Examples   briskly   leisurely   hurriedly   joyfully

Words that describe how **actions** are done are called **adverbs**.

All the adverbs given end with **-ly**, though some adverbs do not.

Example   The doctor did his work **well**.

When **-ly** is added to some words spelling changes are necessary.

Change **y** to **i**   Drop **e**   For others no change is needed

Examples

easy	eas**ily**	gent**l**e	gent**ly**	proud	proud**ly**	careful	careful**ly**
merry	merr**ily**	true	tru**ly**	glad	glad**ly**	truthful	truthful**ly**
heavy	heav**ily**	nob**l**e	nob**ly**	plain	plain**ly**	thankful	thankful**ly**
lucky	luck**ily**	humb**l**e	humb**ly**	quick	quick**ly**	mental	mental**ly**

(A) Write the adverb contained in each of these sentences.

1. The farmer told the hiker plainly what he thought of him.
2. Martin slept soundly all night.
3. The gentleman raised his hat politely.
4. Susan waited patiently for the egg to boil.
5. The bus driver spoke rudely to the old lady.
6. We all laughed heartily at the clowns in the circus.
7. You should always try to speak distinctly.
8. Sally cried bitterly when she broke her new glasses.

(B) Form adverbs from these adjectives, then use any six of them in sentences of your own.

1. rough
2. vain
3. cosy
4. terrible
5. joking
6. equal
7. noisy
8. single
9. mad
10. able
11. haughty
12. loud
13. hasty
14. pitiful
15. sensible
16. nimble

(C) Complete these sentences with a carefully chosen adverb.

1. Roger the dog snored _____.
2. Mrs Jones stomped _____ along the road.
3. James brushed his teeth _____.
4. The baby was red in the face and crying _____.
5. Sam always sings _____.

JOINING SENTENCES WITH RELATIVE PRONOUNS

We found a purse.
It contained money.
(two sentences)

We found a purse **that** *contained money.*
(one sentence)

I have a friend.
He has six tame rabbits.
(two sentences)

I have a friend **who** *has six tame rabbits.*
(one sentence)

Use **who** for persons and **that** for things.

Who and **that** are relative pronouns.

A Use **who** or **that** to join each pair of sentences.

1. Mr Dale has two daughters. They are very much alike.
2. James found the book. Richard had lost it.
3. The police were looking for a man. He had set fire to a factory.
4. Lata was given a ring. It had belonged to her grandmother.
5. David and I met a soldier. He had been awarded the VC.
6. At the museum we saw a uniform. It had been worn by Lord Nelson.
7. Mr and Mrs Harris adopted the two children. They had no one to care for them.
8. Androcles approached the lion. It had a thorn in its paw.

B Complete these sentences.

1. My next-door neighbour has married a man who ....
2. Sally was given a doll that ....
3. It's a story that ....
4. James is the kind of friend who ....

ADJECTIVES

Adjectives are very important words because they describe people and things, and so help us to get a picture of them in our minds.

This is R. L. Stevenson's description of Long John Silver.

"He was very **tall** and **strong**, with a face as **big** as a ham – **plain** and **pale**, but **intelligent** and **smiling**."

Notice the adjectives used:

tall *pale*
strong *intelligent*
big *smiling*
plain

Look at these examples:

a **low**, **thatched** cottage
a **tall**, **handsome** man
fair, **glossy**, **wavy** hair

A Use one adjective to describe each of these nouns.

1. a _____ armchair
2. a _____ dress
3. a _____ school
4. a _____ lamb
5. a _____ nose
6. _____ hair
7. a _____ coat
8. a _____ temper
9. a _____ smell
10. a _____ sky

B Copy these ten nouns into your exercise book, then write two suitable adjectives after each.

1. story
2. food
3. sea
4. path
5. tree
6. friend
7. weather
8. sailor
9. flower
10. beach

C Copy these ten adjectives into your exercise book, then write a suitable noun after each.

1. a thrilling
2. a perilous
3. a nimble
4. a wealthy
5. a brave
6. a sturdy
7. a fertile
8. a faint
9. a glossy
10. a loyal

PROVERBS

A proverb is a **wise saying** that has been in use for hundreds of years.

Learn these proverbs and their meanings.

Penny wise, pound foolish.	People who worry about small details fail to achieve anything worthwhile.
Absence makes the heart grow fonder.	Being separated from someone can make you like him or her all the more.
The early bird catches the worm.	People who arrive early are likely to be better off that those who come late.
Don't count your chickens before they are hatched.	Don't be too confident about possible gains.
Too many cooks spoil the broth.	Too many helpers often get in one another's way.
Empty vessels make most noise.	Ignorant people usually talk more than wise people.
Make hay while the sun shines.	Make the most of your opportunities when they come.
Look before you leap.	Think well before taking any serious step.

(A) Proverbs can seem to contradict each other. Which proverbs in the list above are these four proverbs contradicting?

1 Many hands make light work.
2 Look after the pence and the pounds will look after themselves.
3 He who hesitates is lost.
4 Out of sight, out of mind.

(B) Try to explain in your own words the meaning of these proverbs.

1 A stitch in time saves nine.
2 Better late than never.
3 More haste, less speed.
4 A bird in the hand is worth two in the bush.

HOMOPHONES: SAME SOUND, DIFFERENT MEANING

Some words are pronounced like others but are different in spelling and meaning.			
beat	to strike; a policeman's round; to win, overcome	**need**	to be in want of
		knead	to work up dough
beet	a vegetable	**peal**	a long, loud sound
		peel	the skin of fruit
cell	a small room	**ring**	to sound a bell; a circle
sell	to exchange for money		
feat	a skilful deed	**wring**	to squeeze and twist
feet	plural of foot	**time**	minutes, hours, etc.
bow	to bend low; front of a ship	**thyme**	a herb
		yoke	wooden frame for oxen; part of a dress
bough	a branch		
hall	a large room; a large building	**yolk**	yellow part of an egg
haul	to pull		

A Choose the word that will complete each sentence.

1 A crowd saw Sussex _____ Kent by fifty runs.
2 The cook separated the _____ of the egg from the white.
3 There was a merry _____ of bells as the bridal couple left the church.
4 The man bumped his head on a low _____ of a tree.
5 The prisoner sat in his _____ thinking of his family.

B Use one pair of words from the list above to complete each of the sentences below.

1 At sunset they _____ down the Union Jack on the town _____ flagstaff.
2 Bakers _____ not _____ dough by hand today; machines can do the work.
3 Autumn is the _____ to gather _____ from the garden.
4 Gloria took the _____ off her finger before starting to _____ the clothes.
5 William walked for two hours for charity with blistered _____, which was a remarkable _____ for a boy of ten.

DOCTOR GOLDSMITH'S MEDICINE

Oliver Goldsmith, the author, who was sometimes called Dr Goldsmith because he had studied medicine, gave away so much to the poor that he had little money left for himself.

One day a poor woman called at his house and asked him if he would come to see her husband who was sick and would not eat any food. When Goldsmith called on the family he found that they were very poor because the man had had no work for a considerable time. He discovered that there was no food in the house.

"Come and see me this evening," said Goldsmith to the wife, "and I will let you have some medicine for your husband."

When the woman called that evening Goldsmith gave her a small box which was quite heavy for its size.

"This is the medicine," he explained. "See that it is properly used and it will do your husband the world of good. But please do not open the box until you get home."

"What are the directions for taking it?" asked the woman.

"You will find full directions inside the box," he replied.

Immediately on reaching home the woman sat down beside her husband and opened the box very carefully. It was full of money, on top of which was a slip of paper bearing the words:

"To be taken as often as necessity requires."

Once again Oliver Goldsmith had given away his money to help the poor.

1. Why was Goldsmith sometimes called Doctor although he was really an author?
2. Why did he have little money left for himself?
3. What did the poor woman who called on Goldsmith ask him to do?
4. Why was the woman's family so poor?
5. What did Goldsmith tell the woman to do?
6. What did Goldsmith give the woman that evening?
7. What did Goldsmith ask the woman not to do?
8. Where did Goldsmith tell the woman she would find directions for taking the medicine?
9. What 'medicine' did the box contain?
10. Explain the 'directions' in your own words.

DIRECT AND INDIRECT SPEECH

> "**Don't forget your lunch**, Alan," *said his mother.*
>
> Here we have the actual words spoken by Alan's mother **directly** to him. This is called **direct speech**.
>
> If you heard what Alan's mother had said to him, then went out and told someone else, you would probably say:
>
> *Alan's mother told him not to forget his lunch.*
>
> You would not use her **actual words**.
>
> This is called **indirect speech**.
>
> *Example*
>
> *"It is time you were in bed, Carol," said her mother.* For **direct speech**, speech marks or inverted commas " " are needed.
>
> *Carol's mother told her it was time she was in bed.* For **indirect speech**, speech marks are not needed.

A Change these sentences to **indirect speech**.

1. "The days are getting longer," remarked Mr Findlay.
2. "Have you trimmed the hedges, John?" asked Mrs Gray.
3. "I'm late because of the rain," explained Ramu.
4. "Go on, have another sweet, Michael," urged Sam.
5. "Put the kettle on, Alison," said her mother.
6. "Don't go skating on the pond, Matt," warned his father.

B Change these sentences from **indirect** to **direct speech**.

Example

Charles asked if anybody had seen his exercise book.
"Has anybody seen my exercise book?" asked Charles.

1. Nicholas told his mother that he was really tired.
2. The landlady remarked that it was a glorious day.
3. Ian told Stephen that he was going to have his dinner.
4. David's teacher told him that she expected better work from him in future.
5. The head teacher announced that he would be leaving at the end of the term.
6. Jayant asked Anna if she would like to go to the cinema with him.

ABBREVIATIONS

There is a short way of writing some words.

Examples

Mr is short for **Mister**.   **Rd**. is short for **Road**.

These shortened forms of words are called **abbreviations**.

Sometimes the abbreviations are the shortened forms of foreign words.

am	before noon (*ante meridiem* in Latin)	**IOU**	I owe you
		kph	kilometres per hour
BBC	British Broadcasting Corporation	**MP**	Member of Parliament
		no.	number
cm.	centimetre centimetres	**pm**	afternoon (*post meridiem* in Latin)
cont.	continued	**PC**	police constable
DIY	do it yourself	**PS**	postscript at the end of a letter (*postscriptum* in Latin)
e.g.	for example (exempli gratia in *Latin*)		
etc.	and other things (*et cetera* in Latin)	**RSVP**	please reply (*Répondez s'il vous plaît* in French)

(A) What do these abbreviations stand for?

1 cont.   4 e.g.   7 kph   10 PS
2 MP   5 BBC   8 am   11 PC
3 pm   6 etc.   9 DIY   12 no.

(B) Give the meaning of the abbreviation in bold type in each sentence.

1 You should write to your **MP** about this.
2 The worm was 10 **cm.** long.
3 The new supermarket has a fine selection of fruit, vegetables, groceries, **etc**.
4 The new play will be televised by the **BBC**.
5 The car was travelling at about 80 **kph**.
6 Annette lives at **No.** 8 Church Road.
7 The bank opens at 10 **am**.
8 **PC** West took down full details of the accident.
9 The train leaves at 4.25 **pm**.
10 A new **DIY** store has opened in our town.

(C) Find out what these abbreviations stand for. Your dictionary will be a useful reference source.

1 C. of E.   2 EU   3 NHS   4 UK   5 RSPCA

USING WORDS CORRECTLY

> **Whose** means **belonging to whom**.
> **Who's** means **who is**.
>
> **Began** needs no helping word.
> **Begun** needs a helping word.
>
> **Broke** needs no helping word.
> **Broken** needs a helping word.
>
> **Came** needs no helping word.
> **Come** is used with a helping word here.

(A)
1 Do you know ____ bag this is?
2 I wonder ____ on duty in the library today.
3 The doctor was attending a patient ____ arm was broken.
4 The club leader wants to know ____ responsible for the damage.
5 The woman ____ purse was stolen reported it to the police.

(B)
1 Lessons ____ promptly at nine o'clock.
2 Lessons had ____ when Ahmed arrived at school.
3 Marva has ____ to take a pride in her appearance.
4 Work on the new road was ____ yesterday.
5 Workmen ____ work on the new road yesterday.

(C)
1 A cricket ball ____ the office window.
2 The office window has been ____ several times before.
3 Only two eggs were ____ out of six hundred.
4 A careless packer ____ those two eggs.
5 Lee admitted that he had ____ the ruler.
6 He ____ it when he hit James with it.

(D)
1 The dormouse did not venture out till spring had ____.
2 Has the post ____ yet?
3 Yes, it ____ half an hour ago.
4 I hope you will ____ to my party.
5 You ____ to my party last year.

ALPHABETICAL ORDER

Look at these words:

*sta*ge   *sta*ff   *sta*in   *sta*b   *sta*ck

Notice that the first three letters of each word are the same: **sta**.

To arrange them in alphabetical order we must look at the **fourth** letter of each.

These are:

g f i b c

Letters in alphabetical order:

b c f g i

Words in alphabetical order:

*sta*b   *sta*ck   *sta*ff   *sta*ge   *sta*in

Arrange the words in each group in alphabetical order.

(A) In these groups look at the **first** letter.

1 handsome	print	**2** linger	bathe	**3** quiz	record
wheel	tiger	damage	manage	gloom	flour

(B) In these groups look at the **second** letter.

4 violet	vanish	**5** affect	addition	**6** luggage	leave
vulgar	vestry	ancient	active	light	loyal
vowel		abroad		laugh	

(C) In these groups look at the **third** letter.

7 blink	blank	**8** chilly	chorus	**9** splash	spend
blunder	block	church	cheat	spice	spring
bleak		change		sponge	

(D) Arrange each group in alphabetical order.

1 heave	head	**4** clever	clench	**7** drug	drunk
heath	health	clergy	clean	drum	drudge
2 parent	park	**5** brawn	bracket	**8** strong	street
part	parcel	bramble	branch	struck	stripe
3 recruit	recent	**6** when	where	**9** exclaim	excess
recall	recipe	whether	wheel	exchange	excite

SYNONYMS

	Synonym		Synonym		Synonym
abandon	leave	enormous	huge	squander	waste
abundant	plentiful	fortunate	lucky	sufficient	enough
assist	help	insolent	cheeky	summit	top
cautious	careful	obstinate	stubborn	vacant	empty
celebrated	famous	pathetic	pitiful	vanish	disappear
centre	middle	reckless	rash	wealthy	rich
conceal	hide	slender	slim		

A Copy these sentences, using a simpler word for each word in bold type.

1 Sir David is a **wealthy** banker.
2 I will **assist** you in the shop.
3 The house has been **vacant** for months.
4 He was **fortunate** to escape with slight injuries.
5 Simon did his best to **conceal** the ball he had stolen.
6 When we reached the **summit** of the mountain we rested.
7 There was an **enormous** swelling on the boxer's forehead.
8 The garage was in the **centre** of the town.
9 Apples are **abundant** in the autumn.
10 There was **sufficient** petrol in the car for a long run.

B Explain the difference in meaning of the words in the pairs below.

1 crowd and mob
2 old and antique
3 look and glance
4 cry and sob
5 tired and exhausted

C Give a simpler word for each of these words. Use your dictionary if you wish.

1 comprehend
2 odour
3 remedy
4 intimidate
5 courteous

Old

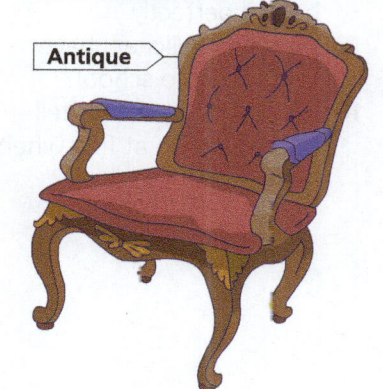
Antique

MICHAEL AT THE CLINIC

Michael followed his mother into the clinic, where a red haired nurse took his name. She remarked that Doctor would probably discharge him today. Michael's scowl returned. "Hope he doesn't," he muttered. The nurse left him scuffing his shoes against the bar of a chair in the waiting room.

Presently his turn came to go into the surgery. Another nurse took off his jacket. A white-coated doctor felt his left arm. He made him turn his wrist from side to side. "Now waggle your fingers and thumb," he said gripping Michael's arm. It did not hurt at all, but Michael managed a convincing "Oow!" and pulled his arm away.

Doctor was not taken in. He smiled at Mother. "Last week's X-rays show that the cracked bone has healed perfectly," he said "Your boy won't have any more trouble with it, Mrs Blake." He took Michael's jacket from Nurse and helped him into it. "Let me see," he said pleasantly, "this is Whit week half-term. School reopens on Monday. Back you go, young man. You must be careful of your arm at first. Otherwise you're as fit as a fiddle."

Michael and the Music Makers   Harry Fleming

1 Who took Michael's name at the clinic?
2 What remark did this person make?
3 What effect did this remark have on Michael?
4 What was Michael doing when the nurse left him?
5 What did the doctor make Michael do with his wrist?
6 What did the doctor tell Michael to do when he gripped his arm?
7 What had been the matter with Michael's arm?
8 How did the doctor know that Michael's arm had healed perfectly?
9 When did Michael have to go back to school?
10 What did the doctor tell Michael to do at first when he returned to school?

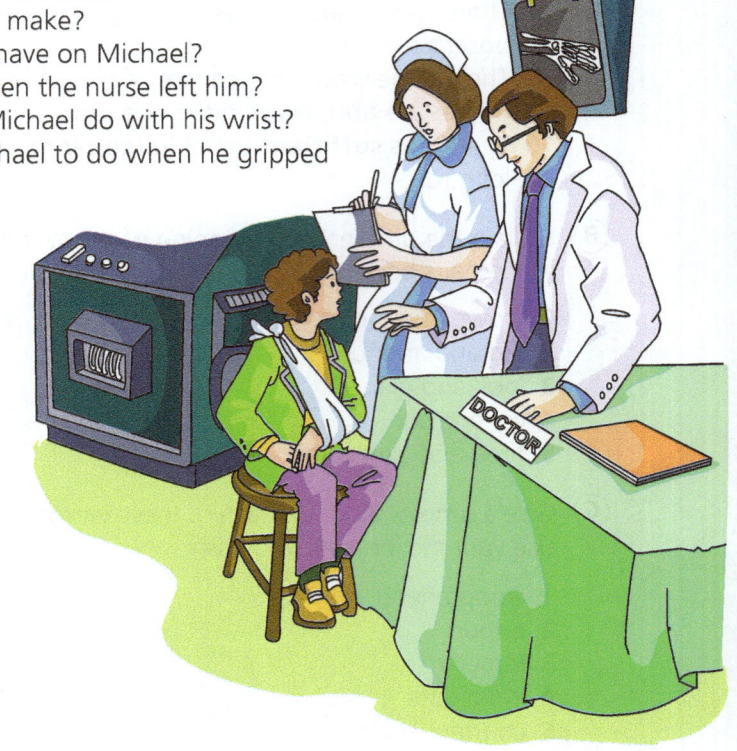

JOINING SENTENCES: CONJUNCTIONS

Jill ate her supper.
She *went to bed.*
            (two sentences)

*Jill ate her supper **and** went to bed.*
            (one sentence)

Ian looked everywhere for his cap.
He *could not find it.*

*Ian looked everywhere for his cap **but** could not find it.*

The words below are all conjunctions. You can use them to join sentences.

or	and	that	before	because
if	but	while	unless	although

Ⓐ Use **and** to join each pair of sentences.

1. Katy washed the car.
   She polished it until it shone.

2. John took off his shoes and socks.
   John paddled in the sea.

3. The goalkeeper jumped high.
   He punched the ball away.

Ⓑ Use **but** to join each pair of sentences.

1. The dog chased the cat.
   He failed to catch her.

2. She slipped and fell.
   She did not hurt herself.

3. Fire destroyed the factory.
   No lives were lost.

Ⓒ Complete each sentence with the correct conjunction, chosen from the list above.

1. She tried the hat on _____ it was too small.
2. The wounded soldier was cheerful _____ he was in pain.
3. I shall be cross _____ you tell me the truth.
4. He was absent from school _____ he had a bad cold.
5. The collector took Janet's ticket _____ punched it.
6. I will come to see you _____ you go abroad.
7. You may come with me _____ you promise to be good.
8. The girls watched television _____ their mother went to the dentist.
9. It was so cold _____ the ponds were frozen.
10. Don't tease the dog _____ it will bite you!

DIRECT SPEECH

Look carefully at the way this conversation is set out.

"What have you been doing?" asked Mrs Green.

"Nothing, Mum," said James.

"What do you mean by 'nothing'?" asked Mrs Green suspiciously.

"Nothing," repeated James, looking a little nervous.

"Nothing?"

Do you see how what Mrs Green says is kept separate from what James says?

Always start a **new line** for a **new speaker**, even if only one word is spoken.

A Copy out these conversations, taking a new line for each new speaker.

1. "Would anyone like an ice-cream?" asked Mrs Green. "Yippee!" yelled James. "Does that mean that you would like one?" smiled his mother. "It means he doesn't want one," said his sister.
2. "That's my chair!" sulked Janine. "Nonsense! I've been sitting in it all morning," retorted Anna. "Exactly!" said Janine. "It's my turn now."
3. "Adam, how do you spell 'minute'?" asked Miss Payne. "I don't know, Miss," said Adam. "Please, Miss, I know," boasted Lynda. "Be quiet, Lynda. I want Adam to have a try."

B Write out this conversation, putting in all the punctuation that is needed and arranging it correctly.

its your turn to feed the rabbits paula told ben its not replied ben it is insisted paula how can it be my turn i fed them yesterday protested ben

C Write a conversation between two friends who are having an argument. Remember to take a new line for each new speaker.

FORMING ABSTRACT NOUNS FROM VERBS

Verb	Noun	Verb	Noun	Verb	Noun
act	action	discover	discovery	marry	marriage
allow	allowance	employ	employment	obey	obedience
arrive	arrival	grow	growth	press	pressure
behave	behaviour	hate	hatred	produce	production
defend	defence	judge	judgement	remain	remainder
defy	defiance	know	knowledge	succeed	success
deliver	delivery				

A Write the missing abstract nouns formed from the verbs in bold type.

1. a generous _____ **allow**
2. a strong _____ **defend**
3. prompt _____ **deliver**
4. complete _____ **obey**
5. a hasty _____ **act**
6. a recent _____ **arrive**
7. a happy _____ **marry**
8. a British _____ **produce**
9. great _____ **press**
10. a huge _____ **succeed**

B Write the abstract noun, formed from the verb in bold type, that will complete each sentence.

1. The children's _____ at the pantomime was excellent. **behave**
2. The dog gobbled up the _____ of the turkey. **remain**
3. Bruce read about the _____ of America by Christopher Columbus. **discover**
4. We watched the _____ of the plant with interest. **grow**
5. Richard has a _____ of brussels sprouts. **hate**

C Write the abstract nouns formed from these verbs. Use your dictionary to help you.

1. add
2. amuse
3. compare
4. conclude
5. decide
6. encourage
7. explain
8. improve
9. introduce
10. punish

VERBS: PAST TENSE AND PAST PARTICIPLES

Present tense	Past tense	Past participle
buy	bought	bought
kneel	knelt	knelt
mow	mowed	mown
saw	sawed	sawn
sew	sewed	sewn
spring	sprang	sprung
swear	swore	sworn
swell	swelled	swollen
tread	trod	trodden
wind	wound	wound

Remember that a past participle needs an auxiliary verb (a helping word).

Example
The patient's arm **had swollen** during the night.

The word **had** helps the participle **swollen**.

*Many vintage cars and motorcycles **have been bought** by the museum.*

The words **have been** help the participle **bought**.

Write the form of the verb in bold type, **past tense** or **past participle**, that will fill each space.

1. Kevin _____ the alarm clock this evening.   **wind**
2. The woodman rested when he had _____ all the wood.   **saw**
3. Bryony _____ the skirt by hand.   **sew**
4. Robert _____ both lawns yesterday.   **mow**
5. Birungi feared that her kitten would be _____ on.   **tread**
6. These gloves were _____ by hand.   **sew**
7. Samran _____ to say his prayers.   **kneel**
8. The old boat had _____ a leak and was sinking.   **spring**
9. The tiger _____ at the daring hunter.   **spring**
10. Both of the scouts had been _____ to secrecy.   **swear**
11. The river was _____ by the torrential rain.   **swell**
12. Mrs Boyce _____ a winter coat in the sale.   **buy**

FUN WITH WORDS

A In the groups below, the second word of each pair is formed by writing a letter **after** the first word. A different letter is used for each group. Look at the letter that is added and write the missing words.

Example bar   bare   bar   bare
fin   fine   fin   fine
hop   ____   hop   hop**e**

In this group the letter **e** is added. What letter is added in the following groups?

1 rip   ripe   4 tea   team   7 pin   pink
   ton   tone   war   warm   for   fork
   wag   ____   fir   ____   bun   ____

2 for   fort   5 bat   bath   8 ban   band
   ten   tent   was   wash   her   herd
   hear ____   clot ____   grin ____

3 sea   seal   6 bee   beer   9 win   wing
   knee kneel   pea   pear   ran   rang
   ear   ____   boa   ____   son   ____

B In each group the second word is formed by changing one of the letters of the first word. Find the letter to be changed in each group, then write the missing words.

Example harp   hard   har**p**   har**d**
slip   slid   sli**p**   sli**d**
steep ____   stee**p** stee**d**

In this group the letter **p** is changed to a **d**. What letter is added in the following groups?

1 bard   bird   4 mix   six   7 bald   bale
   farm   firm   mail   sail   ward   ware
   grand ____   mole   ____   find   ____

2 part   port   5 lone   long   8 bore   sore
   last   lost   pane   pang   bend   send
   came   ____   thine ____   blink ____

3 shot   spot   6 bone   bore   9 hung   lung
   shin   spin   mane   mare   heap   leap
   shade ____   bind   ____   harder ____

SIR HENRY SPRINGS A VISIT

Time and again Ben returned to the Spanish Steps. They were near the hotel, ideal for spare hours when he dared not be absent too long. His favourite place was at the very top, with the street and church behind him and the western skyline, with the Vatican and the long Janiculum ridge, stretched out in front.

There was always so much life and movement there. People streamed up and down like the angels on Jacob's Ladder, endlessly. There were a hundred and thirty-seven steps. He had counted them. If he saw an interesting character toiling up, he could rely on that person pausing for a few minutes at the top. There was usually time for at least a lightning sketch.

Frankly, too, as he had heard men say in Covent Garden Market, it was a good pitch. He sold several sketches there.

He would have sold another – but for Sir Henry. An interested German tourist was already hovering at his elbow, but the drawing was fated to remain in the book, with Ben's methodical note, "Unfinished Flower Girl, Rome, Feb. 14, 1815." Suddenly Sir Henry exploded behind them.

"You young devil! So it's true!"

Ben sprang to his feet and turned. Sir Henry was just dismounting from Lord Frederick's crested carriage, which had pulled up in front of the church door. Lord Frederick and Sir Rupert Dodds were watching amusedly.

"I beg your pardon, sir. You were requiring me?"

"I was told I'd likely find you here. Gad, a servant of mine! Hawking goods in the street like a cheapjack! My friends will be asking, don't I pay you enough?"

Violet for Bonaparte Geoffrey Trease

1 In which year is this story set?
2 For what reason did Ben choose to work at the Spanish Steps?
3 What could Ben see from his favourite place at the top?
4 What made the Steps an ideal place for an artist to work?
5 What do you think is meant by a "lightning sketch"?
6 What occupation had Ben besides being an artist?
7 Which sketch had the tourist been about to buy?
8 Why was Sir Henry so angry about finding Ben there?

PARAGRAPH TOPICS

> **A paragraph is a sequence of sentences about the same topic (subject).**
>
> Read the paragraph below. What is the topic?
>
> *Rhona had an interesting face. Her eyes were very dark and intense and there was a little frown between her eyebrows when she was concentrating. Her nose was uptilted and her mouth and chin were very determined.*
>
> The topic of this paragraph is 'Rhona's interesting face'.

(A) What is the topic of each of these paragraphs?

1. My father worked in a grocer's shop when he first left school. Then, when the war started, he joined the army (and hated every minute of it). When he was demobbed, he had the chance of being trained as a bricklayer. He eventually had his own building firm.
2. Jill's hobby is collecting buttons. She has buttons of all shapes and sizes and colours. She spends hours mounting them carefully on to black card, and they look very beautiful. It's a hobby she's had for years.
3. Lots of people in our class have pets. Four people have hamsters. Three people have goldfish. James says he has a scorpion (but no one else has ever seen it). The most popular pet is a dog – ten people have dogs as pets.
4. Many different types of flower grow in my garden. In the spring there are daffodils and tulips. In the summer there are roses and delphiniums. In the autumn there are chrysanthemums. All year round there are dandelions!

(B) Write a paragraph of four or five sentences about each of these topics.

1. the furniture in your bedroom
2. one of your hobbies
3. your appearance at this moment

ADJECTIVES

| deadly | fragile | boundless | celebrated | strenuous |
| rugged | tarnished | wholesome | forbidding | frequent |

A Copy the adjectives in column **a** in your book, then write after each adjective the noun in column **b** that matches it.

a	b
mountainous	flower
scorching	pupil
deafening	tiger
shabby	mother
fragrant	voice
gigantic	heat
intelligent	clothes
hoarse	country
ferocious	shout
devoted	skyscraper

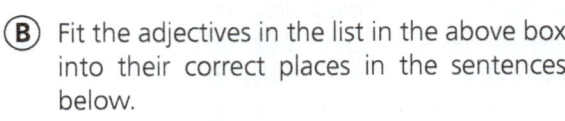

B Fit the adjectives in the list in the above box into their correct places in the sentences below.

1. To be healthy we must eat ____ food.
2. Storms are ____ here in autumn.
3. Some plants contain a ____ poison.
4. Cornwall has a very ____ coastline.
5. We did some ____ exercises to try to lose weight.
6. A large audience heard the recital by the ____ pianist.
7. Securely packed in a box of straw was a ____ china ornament.
8. They were cleaning the ____ silver.
9. The girl's face fell when she saw the ____ look on the face of her teacher.
10. The inventor was a man of ____ energy.

C Use these adjectives in sentences of your own, one sentence for each adjective.

gorgeous	insolent
obstinate	hideous
efficient	accurate
colossal	candid

RHYMES

| hills | miles | curled | flow | breast | tree |
| mills | isles | world | go | dressed | me |

A In the list above are six pairs of rhyming words.
Fit them into their correct places in the verses below.

Great, wide, beautiful, wonderful _____, 1
With the wonderful water round you _____, 2
And the wonderful grass upon your _____ 3
World, you are beautifully _____. 4

The wonderful air is over _____, 5
And the wonderful wind is shaking the _____, 6
It walks on the water, and whirls the _____, 7
And talks to itself on the tops of the _____. 8

You friendly earth! how far do you _____, 9
With the wheat-fields that nod, and the rivers that _____, 10
With cities and gardens, and cliffs and _____ 11
And people upon you for thousands of _____? 12

B Write the words that will complete these sentences. Each word rhymes with the word in bold type in the same line.

Example   **1 please**   missing word is **freeze**

1 In winter the ponds and rivers sometimes _____. **please**
2 A police car soon arrived at the _____ of the accident. **queen**
3 Instead of improving his writing gets _____. **purse**
4 The robins ate every _____ of bread. **slum**
5 The duchess wore a long velvet _____. **poke**
6 In spring the farmers _____ their fields. **mow**

C Write the following as six lines of poetry.

In the dark and lonely night, when the stars are all alight, sleep comes creeping up the street with her naked, silent feet, carrying upon her back dreams of all kinds in a sack.

HOMONYMS: WORDS WITH MORE THAN ONE MEANING

Some words have more than one meaning.

*The miser was too **mean** to buy himself food.*

Some words **mean** much the same as other words.

check	lock	sound	stamp	swallow
hiding	score	spoke	stone	train

A Use the words in the list above to fill the spaces below. The same word must be used for each pair of sentences.

1. You should _____ the working of every sum.
   Farmer Brown wore a _____ suit.
2. In very cold weather workmen _____ their feet to get warm.
   I put a _____ on the letter and posted it.
3. The _____ arrived at the station an hour late.
   Footballers _____ hard to keep fit.
4. It was quiet; not a _____ was to be heard.
   One apple was damaged; the rest were _____.
5. Leanne's plum had a huge _____ in it.
   A big _____ had broken the classroom window.
6. The two boys were _____ behind the oak tree.
   His father gave him a good _____ for robbing birds' nests.
7. A _____ had built its nest under the eaves.
   His throat was so sore that he could hardly _____.
8. A forward's job is to _____ goals for his side.
   There are twenty in a _____.
9. When people go out they should _____ their doors.
   There were two boats in the canal _____.
10. Nobody _____ a word during the music.
    There is a bend _____ in the front wheel of Kai Man's bicycle.

B Write ten sentences of your own showing how each of these words can have two different meanings.

can	right	trunk
litter	light	

OPPOSITES

	Opposite		Opposite
coward	hero	found	lost
few	many	friend	enemy; foe
first	last	loose	tight
float	sink	narrow	wide; broad
forget	remember	often	seldom

A Write the missing words, which are the opposites of the words in bold type.

1 We watched the tin **float** for some time, then it began to _____.
2 In battle the soldier who was thought to be a **coward** proved himself a _____.
3 He has hundreds of **friends** and no _____.
4 The trousers were too **tight** in the legs and too _____ in the waist.
5 James is usually **first** up and _____ to go to bed.
6 The ring that was **lost** in the morning was _____ in the afternoon.
7 The river was very **narrow** at its source but very _____ at its mouth.
8 Robert **remembered** to post his father's letter but _____ to stick a stamp on the envelope.
9 Jean _____ visits us, but we **seldom** see Sandra.
10 **Many** people seek fame, but _____ find it.

B Write the opposites of these words. Some you will remember from the exercises on page 38.

1 lost
2 smooth
3 friend
4 deep
5 few
6 below
7 last
8 tough
9 tight
10 busy
11 often
12 dead
13 remember
14 cheap
15 wide
16 wise
17 float
18 drunk
19 hero
20 bright

LUCY COMES TO HAGWORTHY

Stepping out onto the platform, Lucy looked around expectantly. Two other people got off the train, but apart from the porter there was no one else to be seen. She picked up the suitcases and began to walk towards the ticket office with a sudden sinking feeling. Surely her father hadn't made a muddle over the day? And then a remembered figure appeared at the flight of steps leading up from the little car park below the station – Aunt Mabel, in the same hairy suit that she had said goodbye in five years ago, peering round short-sightedly, heaving a little as she got her breath back after the climb.

They kissed, awkwardly. The porter took Lucy's cases and produced a crate of bottles and a parcel. Could Miss Clough kindly drop them off at Hagworthy?

The crate and the suitcases quite filled the back of Aunt Mabel's small car. Lucy got into the front seat: obviously there would have been no room for Kester and the girls. No doubt that was why they hadn't come. She glanced sideways at Aunt Mabel, who was hunting for the car keys in a handbag that was a turmoil of gloves, handkerchiefs and pieces of paper. She seemed quite undisturbed by their loss, and she had said none of the conventional things about how Lucy had grown, had she had a good journey, and how was her father. She had simply absorbed her niece, along with the crate and the parcel.

Presently the key was found, on the floor, and they set off.

"I don't imagine you remember the way," said Aunt Mabel, changing gear noisily as they rounded the corner onto the main road.

"You turn left at the cross-roads into a very narrow lane where it's difficult to pass things, and then it's all twisty and up and down for about four miles until the village. There's one bit where you can see the beginning of Exmoor, and your cottage is on the right past the post office and the smith, before you get to the pub."

"Good gracious! I didn't think small children noticed so much. What were you – seven?"

Lucy nodded. They had turned into the lane now, and Aunt Mabel was driving in short bursts, in order, as she explained, to dodge from one passing-place to another, with the minimum time in between.

"The worst thing to meet is the milk-lorry. Quite dreadful – you may have to back half a mile. Caravans are another nightmare."

Lucy laughed. The hedges were almost meeting above the car. Meadowsweet foamed on either side, the smell drifting through the windows. "I thought Kester might be at the station."

Aunt Mabel seemed not to hear. She had slowed up to negotiate a tractor. Lucy had to say it again.

"Kester? Oh, Mrs Lang's lad. You remember him, do you? Yes, he'd be about your age, I suppose."

There was a pause.

"Does he know I'm going to be here for the holidays?"

The Wild Hunt of Hagworthy   Penelope Lively

1. How many people got off the train?
2. Why did Lucy have a "sudden sinking feeling"?
3. How was the car park reached from the station?
4. How long was it since Lucy had seen Aunt Mabel?
5. What physical defect did Aunt Mabel have?
6. Which words tell you that she was probably plump?
7. Why do you think Lucy and Aunt Mabel felt awkward when they kissed?
8. What was Aunt Mabel's full name?
9. What are the two "conventional" questions that Aunt Mabel didn't ask Lucy?
10. Which word tells you that the contents of Aunt Mabel's handbag were all mixed up together untidily?
11. How old was Lucy on her last visit?
12. Why did Aunt Mabel drive in "short bursts" in the lane?
13. Explain why "foamed" is a good verb to use to describe how the meadowsweet looked.
14. Which vehicle did Aunt Mabel have to pass?
15. What was Kester's surname?
16. What impression do you get from the extract of Aunt Mabel as a person? Mention as many points about her as you can.

SUBJECT AND PREDICATE

A sentence has two parts, **subject** and **predicate**.

Subject
This is the person or thing spoken about.
Predicate
This is what is said about the subject.

Examples

Subject	**Predicate**
The little girl	*kissed her mother.*
The tired boy	*sat down on the grass.*
Sheep	*bleat.*

A Divide these sentences into **subject** and **predicate**.

1 A bank of cloud covered the sun.
2 Our new teacher has wavy brown hair.
3 The whole family goes to church on Sundays.
4 The two chimpanzees escaped from the zoo.
5 The rough seas capsized the little boat.

B Pair these **subjects** and **predicates**.

1 The stationmaster   in bad weather.
2 Meat and vegetables   walked on his hind legs.
3 The plane took off   is said to be haunted.
4 The clever dog   explained why the train was late.
5 The lonely cottage   make a satisfying meal.

C Add a suitable **predicate** to these **subjects**.

1 The busy shopkeeper ....
2 A juicy apple ....
3 The racing car ....
4 The roar of a lion ....
5 A bunch of flowers ....

D Write a suitable **subject** before each of these **predicates**.

1 .... had to retire from the race.
2 .... was taken to the police station.
3 .... rowed back to the ship.
4 .... make children very happy.

AGREEMENT OF SUBJECT AND VERB

The subject of a sentence must agree with its verb.

A singular subject requires a **singular verb**.

Example
The **boy plays** football every Saturday.

A plural subject requires a **plural verb**.

Example
The **boys play** football every Saturday.

Always use a **singular verb** with these words:
each, anybody, nobody, everybody, everyone, no one, either, neither

Example
Neither of the two boys **was** to blame.
Nobody likes having to admit a mistake.

Use a **plural verb** when two singular nouns in the subject are joined by **and**.

Example
The dog **and** the cat **are** quite friendly.

Singular	Plural	Singular	Plural	Singular	Plural
does	do	is	are	puts	put
cleans	clean	makes	make	was	were
goes	go	takes	take		
has	have	says	say		

Choose the correct verb from the pair above to complete each sentence.

1 make   makes
   My mother _____ delicious flapjacks.

2 clean   cleans
   She _____ her car regularly.

3 has   have
   Everybody _____ to eat in order to live.

4 do   does
   She _____ her best to improve her spelling.

5 put   puts
   Naveed and Mina always _____ their toys away.

6 make   makes
   The children _____ a noise when they play.

7 take   takes
   Some people _____ their pets on holiday.

8 is   are
   Neither of these two books _____ suitable.

9 do   does
   Some pupils _____ their best to write neatly.

WORDS TO COMPLETE WORDS

A A word of four letters is needed to complete each of the unfinished words in these sentences. Make a list of these four-letter words.

Example **1** card cardigan

1 This woollen _ _ _ _ igan will keep you warm.
2 He scored a _ _ _ _ ury in his very first innings.
3 I have come to the last _ _ _ _ ter in my book.
4 Roger and his _ _ _ _ ner gave a fine exhibition of dancing.
5 The _ _ _ _ oon burst when Tony was blowing it up.
6 The _ _ _ _ ory manufactures a large variety of toys.
7 It did not take the nurse long to _ _ _ _ age the patient's leg.
8 We will start work in _ _ _ _ est next Monday morning.

B This exercise is similar to **A** but the missing words come at the end of the unfinished words.

Example **1** mark remark

1 A spectator passed a rude re _ _ _ _ about the referee.
2 The cowboy put a br _ _ _ _ on his horse.
3 He got the boat at the bar _ _ _ _ price of £250.
4 A re _ _ _ _ of £50 was offered for the return of the lost watch.
5 The parents would not give their con _ _ _ _ to the marriage.
6 The class had to trans _ _ _ _ a French story into English.
7 Strong pillars were needed to sup _ _ _ _ the heavy platform.
8 Pat had an ob _ _ _ _ sheet of cardboard ten centimetres long and six centimetres wide.
9 The prisoner made his es _ _ _ _ by climbing over the prison wall.

HOMOPHONES: SAME SOUND, DIFFERENT MEANING

Learn the spelling and the meaning of each word in the list before attempting the exercise.

Examples

die	to stop living	**right**	opposite of left; correct
dye	to colour or stain	**write**	to form words on a surface
four	one more than three	**stair**	a step
fore	at the front	**stare**	to look with wide eyes
pray	to ask God	**steal**	to take another's property
prey	animal hunted for food	**steel**	a very hard metal
rain	water from the clouds	**wait**	to stay or pause
reign	act of ruling	**weight**	how heavy a thing is
rein	strap which guides a horse	**waist**	part of the body
seam	a join in cloth	**waste**	to make poor use of
seem	to appear to be		

A Use the words in the list on the above to complete these sentences.

1 A horse has _____ legs, two hind legs and two _____ legs.
2 These knives and forks are made of stainless _____.
3 The Second World War broke out in the _____ of George VI.
4 Jenny decided to _____ her red dress black.
5 Two pieces of material can be joined by making a _____.
6 You will _____ a lot of material if you make the dress too loose in the _____.
7 Thousands of people _____ for the peace of the world.
8 Most people _____ with their _____ hand.
9 The film star stopped on the top _____ to _____ at the crowd.

B Write the words that are pronounced like those below but that have a different spelling and meaning.

1 sell	5 beat	9 fur	13 hole	17 him
2 ball	6 peel	10 bow	14 time	18 yolk
3 need	7 great	11 ring	15 been	19 peace
4 leak	8 feet	12 hall	16 flower	20 male

INTERNATIONAL AIRPORT

A modern international airport is a vast complex the size of a small town. Each year, it will process through its system hundreds of thousands of aircraft movements, several million passengers and many tons of freight.

Each aircraft movement is controlled from a tower in which there are air-traffic controllers in charge of all taking-off and landing movements. The controllers have a radio link with all aircraft and monitor their airborne movements by radar. Planes are getting faster and runways are growing longer, and modern airports must have a runway at least 50 metres wide and 4 kilometres long.

To process such huge numbers of people each day an airport must employ a staff of many thousands. Amongst these are ground staff to help people with their enquiries, and customs officials to check that certain goods do not go out of or come into the country without their knowledge. Caterers supply the restaurants and cafeterias, as well as providing pre-packed meals for passengers in flight. Maintenance engineers, whose vital job is to ensure the safety of the aircraft, run into several thousands.

Freight is often handled at a separate terminal, where aircraft are usually specially fitted out. Type of freight varies enormously and may include anything from a gorilla bound for a foreign zoo to gold bullion in transit to an overseas bank.

Air travel increases annually, and airport facilities are continually being extended. Today's international airport, already a scene of endless, teeming activity, promises to be even busier in the future.

1 With what may a modern international airport be compared in size?
2 Explain fully the function of an airport.
3 What is the task of the air-traffic controller?
4 From where does the controller operate?
5 How are airborne planes contacted?
6 In what way does radar assist the controller?
7 What is the task of customs officials?
8 Why do you think meals for passengers in flight are pre-packed?
9 Who is responsible for the safety of the aircraft?
10 In what way do you think aeroplanes are specially fitted out to carry freight?

COMMON SAYINGS

Our language contains thousands of common sayings not found in other languages. It is important to know them and to understand them, for at first sight many of them do not make sense.

Examples

Common saying	Meaning
to hit below the belt	to act unfairly towards an opponent
to have a bone to pick with someone	to have a dispute to settle or a complaint to make
to paddle one's own canoe	to do things for oneself
to put the cart before the horse	to do things the wrong way round
to let the cat out of the bag	to give away a secret
to make both ends meet	to live within one's means
to have a feather in one's cap	to have done something to be proud of
to hang one's head	to be ashamed of oneself
to turn over a new leaf	to lead a new life
to get into hot water	to get into trouble

Complete these sayings and describe a situation where each could apply.

1 to let the _____ out of the _____
2 to get into _____ water
3 to make both _____ meet
4 to paddle one's own _____
5 to have a _____ in one's cap
6 to hit below the _____
7 to _____ one's head
8 to have a _____ to _____ with someone
9 to turn over a new _____
10 to put the _____ before the _____

SYNONYMS

	Synonym		Synonym		Synonym
annual	yearly	generous	kind	purchase	buy
attempt	try	enquire	ask	putrid	rotten
cease	stop	insane	mad	rare	scarce
circular	round	manufacture	make	regret	sorrow
coarse	rough	moist	damp	reply	answer
courageous	brave	necessity	need	scared	frightened
drowsy	sleepy	portion	part		

A Copy the words in column **a**, then opposite each write the word in column **b** that is similar in meaning.

a	b	a	b
enquire	stop	moist	round
necessity	rotten	cease	ask
rare	damp	putrid	part
circular	need	regret	scarce
drowsy	sorrow	portion	sleepy

B In place of each word in bold type write another word that has a similar meaning.

1. Sir Malcolm was thanked for his **generous** gift to the hospital.
2. There will be a big crowd to see the champion driver **attempt** to break the world record next month.
3. I have received no **reply** to my letter.
4. After his huge Sunday lunch Tim felt quite **drowsy**.
5. The material is very **coarse**.
6. People **purchase** warm clothing in readiness for winter.
7. The **annual** Flower Show is held in September.
8. Ann was **scared** of the big bloodhound.

C Explain the difference in meaning between the words in these pairs. Use your dictionary.

1. generous   extravagant
2. hungry   starving
3. unfriendly hostile

WORDS THAT SAVE WORK

One word can sometimes do the work of several.

Example

At the end of the week Adrian was **without a penny**.

At the end of the week Adrian was **penniless**.

annually	briefly	capsized	correctly	decide	died
disappeared	homeless	improving	mad; insane	miser	rescued
returned	soon	suddenly	useless	widow	

A Use one word in place of those in bold type in each sentence. All the labour-saving words are in the list above.

1. The boarding-house was kept by a **woman whose husband was dead**.
2. The lifeboat **saved the lives of** the crew of the sinking ship.
3. The old man **passed away** in his sleep.
4. The manager went to London but **came back again** the next day.
5. As a result of the fire several people were **without a home**.
6. I hope to see you **before very long**.
7. Hari was **of no use** in the garden.
8. The shipwrecked sailor was **out of his mind**.
9. The pickpocket soon **went out of sight**.
10. Mary's writing is **getting better** every day.

B Use the remaining words from the box above to replace the words in bold type in the following sentences.

1. The reporter told his story **in very few words**.
2. Esam could not **make up his mind** which book to buy.
3. Peter worked ten sums **without making a single mistake**.
4. The Welsh National Eisteddfod is held **once every year**.
5. **Without any warning** a policeman appeared on the scene.
6. Nobody admires a **man who hoards his money**.
7. The little boat **turned completely upside down**.

RHYMES

| eat | lurch | neat | thrush | sedge |
| bush | hedge | force | perch | course |

A Write the words from the list above that fill the spaces in the following lines of poetry.

Winter

Sweet blackbird is silenced with chaffinch and _____, **1**
Only waistcoated robin still chirps in the _____; **2**
Soft sun-loving swallows have mustered in _____, **3**
And winged to the spice-teeming southlands their _____. **4**
Plump housekeeper dormouse has tucked himself _____, **5**
Just a brown ball in moss with a morsel to _____: **6**
Armed hedgehog has huddled him into the _____, **7**
While frogs scarce miss freezing deep down in the _____. **8**
Soft swallows have left us alone in the _____, **9**
But robin sits whistling to us from his _____. **10**

B Each of the words missing from these sentences rhymes with the word in bold type.

  1 The full-back was penalized for _____ play.   **howl**
  2 He _____ every word he said.   **tent**
  3 After the match crowds swarmed on to the _____.   **healed**
  4 I _____ if I shall be able to come.   **shout**
  5 Samantha _____ the ball that Kerry threw to her.   **port**
  6 This room requires a new _____ of furniture.   **beat**

C The three words in each group rhyme with the word in bold type. Write the rhyming words.

1 late
  w _____
  aw _____
  cr _____

2 rain
  cr _____
  ch _____
  sk _____

3 share
  desp _____
  decl _____
  sw _____

4 bite
  fr _____
  h _____
  sp _____

5 bean
  cant _____
  mach _____
  sc _____

NOISES OF CREATURES

| hum | cackle | hiss | squeak | caw | howl |
| coo | neigh | | whinny | hoot | hiss |

A Write the names of the noises made by the creatures in the pictures. You learned them in Book 2.

B Look at the list above, then write the missing words.

1 wolves _____
2 mice _____
3 geese _____
4 owls _____
5 snakes _____
6 _____ hum
7 _____ caw
8 _____ coo

C Write the words needed to complete these sentences. Add **-ing** or **-ed** to your words where required.

1 From the woods came the _____ of doves.
2 The _____ of the mice stopped when the cat entered.
3 The _____ of owls in the old ruins disturbs my sleep.
4 The ducks _____ loudly as they waddled to the pond.
5 What could be more unmusical than the _____ of rooks?
6 The hunter sprang backwards when the snake _____.
7 The silence of the night was suddenly shattered by the _____ of wolves.
8 Bees were _____ as they flew from flower to flower.
9 As the farmer's wife appeared the geese began to _____.
10 The racehorse _____ with joy as the stable boy approached with its feed.

A MAD TEA-PARTY

There was a table set out under a tree in front of the house, and the March Hare and the Hatter were having tea at it: a Dormouse was sitting between them, fast asleep, and the other two were using it as a cushion, resting their elbows on it, and talking over its head "Very uncomfortable for the Dormouse," thought Alice: "only as it's asleep, I suppose it doesn't mind."

The table was a large one, but the three were all crowded together at the one corner of it: "No room! No room!" they cried out when they saw Alice coming.

"There's *plenty* of room!" said Alice indignantly, and she sat down in a large arm-chair at one end of the table.

"Have some wine," the March Hare said in an encouraging tone.

Alice looked all round the table, but there was nothing on it but tea. "I don't see any wine," she remarked.

"There isn't any," said the March Hare.

"Then it wasn't very civil of you to offer it," said Alice angrily.

"It wasn't very civil of you to sit down without being invited," said the March Hare.

"I didn't know it was *your* table," said Alice; "it's laid for a great many more than three."

"Your hair wants cutting," said the Hatter. He had been looking at Alice for some time with great curiosity, and this was his first speech.

"You should learn not to make personal remarks," Alice said with some severity; "it's very rude."

The Hatter opened his eyes very wide on hearing this; but all he said was, "Why is a raven like a writing desk?"

"Come, we shall have some fun now!" thought Alice.

Alice's Adventures in Wonderland   Lewis Carroll

1 Who was sitting at the table under the tree when Alice arrived?
2 What were the March Hare and Hatter resting their elbows on?
3 What did the March Hare offer Alice?
4 Why didn't she take any?
5 List three ways in which Alice spoke to her hosts.
6 Why was Alice angry with the March Hare?
7 Was the Hatter mad or angry or both? Give reasons for your answer.
8 Why does Alice think they will have fun now?

SOUNDS

Learn the names of the sounds made by the objects in the list below. Some of the words you learned in Book 2.

Object	Sound	Object	Sound
bugle	call	paper	rustle, crackle
rain	patter	saw	buzz
feet	tramp; shuffle	steam	hiss
gun	boom	telephone	ringing
hoofs	thunder; clatter	whistle	shriek

Write the missing words.

A
1 the ringing of a _____
2 the buzz of a _____
3 the patter of _____
4 the hiss of _____
5 the shriek of a _____
6 the rustle of _____
7 the call of a _____
8 the clatter of _____
9 the tramp of _____
10 the boom of a _____

B
1 the _____ of a clock
2 the _____ of dishes
3 the _____ of leaves
4 the _____ of raindrops
5 the _____ of a whip
6 the _____ of the wind
7 the _____ of a drum
8 the _____ of coins
9 the _____ of a door
10 the _____ of a horn

C Write the words needed to complete these sentences.

1 With a _____ of the whistle the express thundered through the little station.
2 The _____ of a bugle summoned the scouts to dinner.
3 The campers heard the _____ of rain on leaves.
4 The _____ of a telephone echoed in the empty hall.
5 There was a _____ of steam as the old locomotive pulled up.
6 With a _____ of hoofs the hunt went in pursuit of the fox.
7 The _____ of feet filled the air as the regiment marched along.
8 There was a loud _____ as the circular saw cut through the thick wood.

ANALOGIES

*The home of a **horse** is called a **stable**.*

*The home of a **dog** is called a **kennel**.*

The **stable** is to the **horse** what the **kennel** is to the **dog** – a home.

We can express it in this way:

Stable is to **horse**
as
kennel is to **dog**;

or

Horse is to **stable**
as
dog is to **kennel**.

A Look at the exercise below. In each line find how the words in each pair are related – homes, gender, opposites, parts of the body, occupations, etc. Then write the missing words.

1 **Horse** is to **stable** as **bee** is to _____.
2 **Man** is to **woman** as **uncle** is to _____.
3 **Big** is to **small** as **wide** is to _____.
4 **Foot** is to **toe** as **hand** is to _____.
5 **Cat** is to **kitten** as **lion** is to _____.
6 **Cow** is to **beef** as **calf** is to _____.
7 **Sheep** is to **wool** as **rabbit** is to _____.
8 **Dog** is to **paw** as **horse** is to _____.

B Write the missing words.

1 **North** is to **south** as _____ is to **west**.
2 **Shoe** is to **foot** as _____ is to **hand**.
3 **Lion** is to **roar** as _____ is to **trumpet**.
4 **Ankle** is to **leg** as _____ is to **arm**.
5 **Car** is to **garage** as _____ is to **hangar**.
6 **February** is to **March** as _____ is to **Wednesday**.
7 **Soldier** is to **army** as _____ is to **navy**.
8 **Picture** is to **artist** as _____ is to **poet**.

THE DOERS OF ACTIONS

Here is a list of twenty actions and the words used for the people who do these actions.

Action	Doer	Action	Doer	Action	Doer
act	actor	cycle	cyclist	reside	resident
apply	applicant	decorate	decorator	sail	sailor
beg	beggar	detect	detective	study	student
canoe	canoeist	inhabit	inhabitant	supply	supplier
climb	climber	invent	inventor	tour	tourist
conquer	conqueror	kidnap	kidnapper	travel	traveller
create	creator	manage	manager		

A What word is used for:

1 one who climbs?
2 one who supplies?
3 one who studies?
4 one who acts?
5 one who detects?
6 one who travels?
7 one who sails?
8 one who begs?
9 one who tours?
10 one who creates?

B Write the words needed to complete these sentences. Look at the words in bold type at the end of each line.

1 The _____ had covered fifty kilometres before noon.   **cycle**
2 Every _____ in the street signed the protest against higher rents.   **reside**
3 The house was papered and painted by a London _____   **decorate**
4 John Logie Baird was the _____ of television.   **invent**
5 There were seven _____ for the post of Head Teacher.   **apply**
6 The _____ of the bank was most helpful.   **manage**
7 The _____ capsized deliberately.   **canoe**
8 Sir Edmund Hillary and Tenzing Norgay were the first _____ of Mount Everest.   **conquer**
9 Mr Giles is the oldest _____ of the village.   **inhabit**
10 A reward was offered for the capture of the _____.   **kidnap**

SENTENCES IN THE CORRECT ORDER

> Each of these stories consists of a number of sentences that are not in their correct order. Show, by using numbers, the order in which they should be.

A

1. Mike: "I suppose the wax candle will."
2. Pat: "Wrong, neither of them; they both burn shorter."
3. Pat: "Which will burn longer, wax candle or a tallow candle?"

B

1. "Of course there is," said his mother, "or why did the little boy burst?"
2. "There's no such thing as too much trifle, Mummy," replied David.
3. "David," said his mother, "did you hear about the little boy who ate too much trifle and burst?"
4. David passed his plate for another helping. "Not enough boy," he chuckled.
5. David started gleefully on his third helping of trifle.

C

1. After a time a wasp landed among the flies and stung him on the nose.
2. "Shoo!" he muttered impatiently. "Since some of you can't behave you must all get off my face."
3. A lazy old tramp lay on the grass in the warm sunshine.
4. At this he raised one dirty hand and rubbed it all over his dirty face.
5. His face was covered with flies, for he was too lazy to drive them off.

D

1. "Well, don't you call that an accident?"
2. A man was being examined by a doctor.
3. "No, sir! He did it on purpose."
4. "Have you ever had an accident?" asked the doctor.
5. "Never, sir," replied the man, "except when a bull tossed me over a fence."

ABBREVIATIONS

Here is another list of abbreviations, or short ways of writing words. Learn them thoroughly, then answer the questions.

AD	In the year of Our Lord (*anno Domini* in Latin)	**HMS**	Her Majesty's Ship
		p	page; pence
BC	Before Christ	**PO**	post office
Capt.	Captain		postal order
dept.	department	**PTO**	please turn over
ETA	estimated time of arrival	**RAF**	royal air force
FA	Football Association	**UFO**	unidentified flying object
HM	Her Majesty	**VIP**	very important person

A Give the meanings of these abbreviations.

1 VIP
2 p.
3 BC
4 dept.
5 HM
6 AD
7 PO
8 Capt.
9 PTO
10 UFO
11 RAF
12 HMS

B What do the abbreviations in these sentences stand for?

1 Julius Caesar invaded Britain in 55 **BC**.
2 Uncle Steve is now serving in **HMS** *Eagle*.
3 **Capt**. Scott commanded the ship *Discovery*, which explored the Antarctic.
4 An amusing cartoon appears on **p**. 25.
5 Big alterations are being carried out in the Toy **Dept**.
6 **HM** the Queen received a rousing welcome.
7 America was discovered in **AD** 1492.
8 Enclosed in the letter was a **PO** for 50p.
9 Mr Gibson is a flying officer in the **RAF**.
10 Please let us know the date you are coming and your **eta**.

DICKON AND MARY

There was a laurel-hedged walk which curved round the secret garden and ended at a gate which opened into a wood in the park. Mary thought she would skip round this walk and look into the wood and see if there were any rabbits hopping about. She enjoyed the skipping very much, and when she reached the little gate she opened it and went through because she heard a low, peculiar whistling sound and wanted to find out what it was.

It was a very strange thing indeed. She quite caught her breath as she stopped to look at it. A boy was sitting under a tree, with his back against it, playing on a rough wooden pipe. He was a funny-looking boy about twelve. He looked very clean and his nose turned up and his cheeks were as red as poppies, and never had Mistress Mary seen such round and such blue eyes in any boy's face. And on the trunk of the tree he leaned against, a brown squirrel was clinging and watching him, and from behind a bush near by a cock pheasant was delicately stretching his neck to peep out, and quite near him were two rabbits sitting up and sniffing with tremulous noses – and actually it appeared as if they were all drawing near to watch him and listen to the strange, low, little call his pipe seemed to make.

When he saw Mary he held up his hand and spoke to her in a voice almost as low as and rather like his piping.

"Don't tha' move," he said. "It'd flight 'em."

Mary remained motionless. He stopped playing his pipe and began to rise from the ground He moved so slowly that it scarcely seemed as though he were moving at all, but at last he stood on his feet and then the squirrel scampered back up into the branches of his tree, the pheasant withdrew his head, and the rabbits dropped on all fours and began to hop away, though not at all as if they were frightened

"I'm Dickon," the boy said. "I know tha'rt Miss Mary."

Then Mary realized that somehow she had known at first that he was Dickon. Who else could have been charming rabbits and pheasants as the natives charm snakes in India? He had a wide, red, curving mouth and his smile spread all over his face.

"I got up slow," he explained, "because if tha' makes a quick move it startles' 'em. A body 'as to move gentle an' speak low when wild things is about."

He did not speak to her as if they had never seen each other before, but as if he knew her quite well. Mary knew nothing about boys, and she spoke to him a little stiffly because she felt rather shy.

"Did you get Martha's letter?" she asked

He nodded his curly, rust-coloured head.

"That's why I come."

He stooped to pick up something which had been lying on the ground beside him when he piped.

"I've got th' garden tools. There's a little spade an' rake an' a fork an' hoe. Eh! They are good 'uns. There's a trowel, too. An' th' woman in th' shop threw in a packet o' white poppy an' one o' blue larkspur when I bought th' other seeds."

"Will you show the seeds to me?" Mary said.

She wished she could talk as he did. His speech was so quick and easy. It sounded as if he liked her and was not the least afraid she would not like him, though he was only a common moor boy, in patched clothes and with a funny face and a rough, rusty-red head. As she came closer to him she noticed that there was a clean fresh scent of heather and grass and leaves about him, almost as if he were made of them. She liked it very much, and when she looked into his funny face with the red cheeks and round blue eyes she forgot that she had felt shy.

The Secret Garden   Frances Hodgson Burnett

1 What does Mary decide to do at the start of this scene?
2 What makes her stop and go through the little gate?
3 Which creatures are near Dickon as he plays on his pipe?
4 What does Dickon mean when he says, "It'd flight 'em"?
5 How can you tell that Mary has heard of Dickon before she sees him?
6 Why does Mary speak stiffly to Dickon?
7 Why has Dickon come to see Mary?
8 What has he brought with him for her?
9 In what way does Dickon speak differently from Mary? Why do you think this is?
10 Write a detailed description of Dickon based on what we are told about him in this passage, but using your own words too.

MORE FUN WITH WORDS

A Rearrange the letters of each word in bold type to complete the sentences.

Example

The **bleat** was made of solid oak.
The **table** was made of solid oak.

1. The famous actress first appeared on the **gates** when she was only six.
2. Captain Smith has a long, brown **bread**.
3. Whilst picking blackberries Paul got a **north** in his finger.
4. Jim helped to pick the ripe **lumps**.
5. A huge **could** darkened the sky.
6. The **plates** of the buttercup are yellow.
7. A large crowd watched the soldiers **charm** through the town.
8. The customer refused to take the **least** loaf of bread.

B In each group below, the second word of each pair is formed by inserting a letter after the first letter of the first word.

Example

cat	coat	cat	coat
lad	load	lad	load
hard	___	hard	hoard

The letter **o** has been inserted.

1. sock smock
   sell smell
   sash ___

2. pay pray
   band brand
   fight ___

3. sake shake
   coke choke
   soot ___

4. fag flag
   beak bleak
   pain ___

5. sand stand
   sick stick
   sole ___

6. sat spat
   send spend
   soil ___

7. bad bead
   fast feast
   cram ___

8. lid laid
   pin pain
   pint ___

9. sum scum
   sold scold
   sent ___

PROVERBS

Learn these proverbs and their meanings before attempting the questions that follow.

Birds of a feather flock together.	People of similar tastes enjoy one another's company.
Cut your coat according to your cloth.	Learn to live within your means.
Fine feathers make fine birds.	Fine clothes make a person look important, although he or she may not be.
Two heads are better than one.	Two people together may solve a problem that one alone cannot.
Waste not, want not.	Be thrifty and you may never be in need.
One good turn deserves another.	People who are kind to others deserve the same treatment themselves.
People who live in glass houses should not throw stones.	Those in a weak position themselves should not attack others.
The proof of the pudding is in the eating.	Judge by results.
Let sleeping dogs lie.	Don't stir up trouble.

Write the proverbs that these sentences suggest.

1 She dresses and looks like a duchess although she is poor.
2 If you earn £50 a week you should not spend more than £50 a week.
3 Perhaps you can help me to solve this problem.
4 Smith, Brown and Johnson are great fr ends; all are keen on music.
5 Carol mended Ian's socks so Ian cooked the lunch.

SIMILES

When something is very **light** in weight we say it is **as light as a feather**.

This is because it is similar to a feather in **weight**.

Learn the sayings in this list, then answer the questions.

as light as a feather
as cunning as a fox
as flat as a pancake
as fresh as a daisy
as old as the hills

as poor as a church mouse
as proud as a peacock
as quick as lightning
as safe as houses
as steady as a rock

A Write the missing words.

1 as steady as a _____
2 as proud as a _____
3 as poor as a _____
4 as flat as a _____
5 as quick as _____

6 as safe as _____
7 as light as a _____
8 as fresh as a _____
9 as old as the _____
10 as cunning as a _____

B What are the missing words?

1 Our cricket field is as flat as a _____.
2 This hat is as old as the _____.
3 The old oak table was as steady as a _____.
4 After losing his fortune Dick was a poor as a _____.
5 His movements were as quick as _____.

C Write the saying that fits each picture.

D Think of some new similes for yourself that describe these situations really well.

1 My sister was as proud as _____ after passing the exam.
2 Even though he was very busy, the shop keeper remained as cool as a _____.
3 She was as mad as a _____.

VARIETY IN WRITING SENTENCES

> Notice the order of words in this sentence.
> ***A ruined castle*** *stood on top of the hill.*
> (subject first)
> You will see that the subject, the thing spoken about, comes first.
> Now look at this sentence.
> *On top of the hill stood a **ruined castle**.*
> (subject last)
> It is natural to put the subject of a sentence first, but by changing this order it is possible to create variety. This makes the writing of sentences much more interesting.

A Rewrite these sentences, beginning with the words in bold type. Don't forget to use a capital letter for the first word.

1. The two boys went to see a film **last** night.
2. The rooks were cawing loudly **up** in the tall trees.
3. My brother decided to become a policeman **because** he is so tall and strong.
4. The carnival was postponed **owing** to the very heavy rain.
5. The village smithy stands **under** a spreading chestnut tree.

B Now do the same with these sentences.

1. Soon after his father died **Michael** emigrated to Canada.
2. Under the railway bridge **a** tramp was sheltering from the rain.
3. Without stopping to look for cars, **Martin** darted across the road.
4. In the nick of time **the** fireman jumped clear of the falling roof.
5. Because he did not work **Roger** failed his exam.

C Write three sentences of your own in which the subject comes first, then rewrite each sentence so that the subject comes last.

D Complete these sentences.

1. Without a word, Joe ....
2. Behind the house there ....
3. Jumping over the gate, the thief ....
4. At the last moment my father ....

THE GOLDEN FLEECE

Immediately the fifty heroes got on board, and, seizing their oars, held them perpendicularly in the air, while Orpheus (who liked such a task far better than rowing) swept his fingers across the harp. At the first ringing note of the music they felt the vessel stir. Orpheus thrummed away briskly, and the galley slid at once into the sea, dipping her prow deeply and rising again as buoyant as a swan. Thus triumphantly did the *Argo* sail out of harbour, amidst the good wishes of everybody except the wicked old Pelias, who stood on a promontory scowling at her, and wishing he could blow out of his lungs the tempest of wrath that was in his heart, and so sink the galley with all on board

To make the time pass more pleasantly during the voyage the heroes talked about the Golden Fleece. It had originally belonged to a ram, who had taken on his back two children, when in danger of their lives, and fled with them over land and sea. One of the children, whose name was Helle, fell into the sea and was drowned. But the other (a little boy named Phrixus) was brought safely ashore by the faithful ram, who, however, was so exhausted that he immediately lay down and died. In memory of this good deed the fleece of the poor dead ram was miraculously changed to gold It was hung upon a tree in a sacred grove, where it had now been kept for many years, and was the envy of mighty kings, who had nothing so magnificent in any of their palaces.

Tanglewood Tales   Nathaniel Hawthorne

1 How many heroes went aboard the *Argo*?
2 What did Orpheus like doing far better than rowing?
3 What did the heroes feel at the first ringing note of the music?
4 What is a **promontory**?
5 What did Pelias wish he could do to the ship?
6 How did the heroes make the time pass more pleasantly during the voyage?
7 How did Helle die?
8 What happened to Phrixus?
9 What change came over the fleece of the ram after its death?
10 Where was the ram's fleece kept?